RENEWING A LOCAL ECONOMY:
THE ENTREPRENEURIAL RESPONSE TO CRISIS

Renewing a Local Economy:

The Entrepreneurial Response to Crisis

CONNELL M. FANNING

Cork University Press
1986

First published in 1986 by
Cork University Press, University College, Cork

British Library Cataloguing in Publication Data
Fanning, Connell M.
Renewing a local economy: the entrepreneurial response to crisis.
1. Cork (County) — Economic conditions
I. Title
330.9419'50824 HC260.5.Z7C6

ISBN 0-902561-37-5

Printed in the Republic of Ireland by Tower Books,
86 South Main St., Cork

To the memory of A.P. and for Clara

Acknowledgements

Over the last two years I have incurred enormous debts to a very large number of people for many hours of discussion and other assistance in examining the unemployment crisis in Cork. Noting names in an acknowledgment list is obviously an inadequate way of expressing gratitude; my only other way is to hope that what is contained herein is of some use in addressing the challenges which face Cork, as well as other areas, in the future.

The number of people who have directly helped with this study and indirectly through some related projects is too large to name all here but the debt due to a number of people who have been particularly helpful ought to be noted explicitly. Four persons have gone far beyond what could even *unreasonably* be expected in the ideas, information, and support they have unhesitatingly given at every call: Jack Casey (Beamish and Crawford Ltd. and President, Cork Chamber of Commerce), Sean McHenry (Vita Cortx Ltd. and IDA Small Industries Board), Joe Mulcahy (Regional Policy DGXVI, European Commission) and David O'Mahony (Dept. of Economics, University College, Cork).

As well as these the following (in order of organizations) also rendered assistance and ideas on different aspects: Liam Fitzpatrick, Barry Murphy and Henry O'Brien (Allied Irish Banks); John Butler, Terry McCarthy and Denis Rowan (AnCO); Curtis Fritze, Jay Kershaw, Ron Smith (Control Data Worldtech Inc); Nicholas Mansergh and John O'Donnell (Cork Corporation); Brendan Kelleher, John McAleer, and David Murphy (Cork County Council); Tony Thornton (Craig Gardner); Agnes Breathnach (Dept. of Industry); Gerry Hughes and Kieran Kennedy (Economic and Social Research Institute); Rory McKenna (European Commission, Brussels); Peter Doyle and Conor Maguire (European Commission, Dublin); Tom Barret, Cathal Kavanagh, Dick Power, and Brian Phillips (European Investment Bank); Denis O'Connell (Industrial Credit Corporation); Denis McCarthy and John Toner (Industrial Development Authority); Tom Carrol (Innovation Centre); Donal Lenihan (Mayfield Enterprise Initiative); Hugh Logue (National Board of Science and

Technology); Phil Duggan and Flor O'Leary (National Manpower Service); Eugene O'Connor (Southern Health Board); Adrian Stokes (Stokes & Co.); Alan Cassells, Joe Lee and Tony Weaver (University College, Cork); A. Gillespie, J. Goddard, D. Storey, and A. Thwaites (University of Newcastle-Upon-Tyne); Michael Banks and Jim Harrington (Worldtech Ventures, Ltd); and Tom Costelloe and Niall Green (Youth Employment Agency).

As well as these many more persons in many more organizations (a few of which are listed in Chapter 4) have contributed to greater or lesser extents which is appreciated although space limitation, or a desire for confidentiality, preclude an explicit acknowledgement here.

Although whatever may be of merit is due primarily to the above, the usual disclaimer, that none of them bear any responsibility for the views or information contained herein, of course fully applies.

Finally, but not, needless to say, least my thanks are due to Anne Begley and Maura McGrath for their assistance and, particularly to Vivienne Murray for her usual efficiency and fortitude in dealing with all the demands made on her skills and patience. Also thanks are due to Donal Counihan, Executive Secretary, Cork University Press and to the Committee of the Cork University Press, as well as Seán Daly, Printer, for facilitating all aspects of the production side of the work and Patricia Kenny for assistance with proofreading and related tasks. Their willingness to do all they could on my behalf cannot include liability for remaining faults.

As always, the patience and understanding of Mary and Saranna were continually demanded and invariably forthcoming.

Contents

When the decline in population occurs through emigration, it is possible — though by no means always certain — that the more enterprising and ambitious people leave the country. Emigration seems also to produce certain attitudes of mind and patterns of behaviour which are prejudicial to economic development. People appear to become mentally disorientated and to become like an uprooted or rootless people even in their own country. This results in a tendency to evade risktaking and responsibility so that even the limited investment opportunities that may exist may not be exploited to the full.

(David O'Mahony. *The Irish Economy.* 1964)

No country more dramatically shows the after-effects of continuous emigration than Ireland. If one wants to see what Algeria, Turkey, or Portugal might well be like in fifty years time, go to Ireland. It should be the migrants crystal ball . . . once emigration reaches endemic proportions (as it has in Ireland) a kind of human depression and social despair sets in.

(J. Power. The New Proletarians. *Encounter.* 1974)

The most serious economic and social problem facing Ireland is the very high level of unemployment. It is also the most intractable problem, and there is widespread despondency regarding the prospects of doing much about it — even in the longer term.

(Denis Conniffe and Kieran A. Kennedy. *Employment and Unemployment Policy for Ireland.* 1984)

Preface

For more than sixty years, as a sovereign state, the Republic of Ireland has faced *an* employment challenge and has failed, except very temporarily during the nineteen sixties, to resolve it without large scale emigration. Indeed, I believe it can be fairly argued that as a society we have never fundamentally addressed, directly or indirectly through our public representatives, this problem and sought to discover and organize the conditions necessary for sustaining a high employment economy with growing real incomes, which are distributed according to generally accepted criteria of merit and need. In recent decades our development policies have relied heavily, and at times it appeared almost totally, on inducing foreign businesses to come to Ireland to 'create jobs' or on borrowing the saved resources of foreigners to provide us with the standard of living which we failed to generate ourselves. Neither of these could provide the basis for a long-term strategy and the brutal realities of the changes in the world economic environment — falling demand, high real interest rates, volatile exchange rates etc. — have made us unforgettably aware of what was implicit, but ignored, during the easier times behind us.

Now there is no doubt that the answer — if there is one — to our employment crisis can only be found within ourselves. We have only begun, under the pressure of the immediate crisis, the process of discovering right ways to meet our needs and aspirations. This small book has developed out of the particular experience of crisis and response in one area, namely, the Cork Greater Urban Area. But because *Cork is not a special case* in the overall employment crisis in Ireland the lessons emerging and approach being discovered in Cork are of direct relevance to areas facing similar challenges. Thus while it makes the exposition more concrete to base it on the Cork situation, with which I am most familiar, I hope that the wider relevance of the experience and type of local response emerging in Cork will also be transparent.

Two qualifications should be made at the outset. The first is that, as the crisis continues and deepens, new developments and 'initiatives' are taking place or being announced all the time by, for example, the various state agencies as they seek to find ways to alleviate the situation. Therefore at some point a halt has to be made in attempting to be current in the coverage of developments. This decision merely complements the earlier one which was concerned with selecting what was to be included anyway. Since the final draft of the book was done in January a number of further matters, specific to Cork, have taken place which it was not possible to integrate properly at a late stage into the study.

In particular two recent items should be mentioned explicitly. These are the Enterprise Centre at the North Mall (outlined in the book), which is currently under construction and due to be completed later this year, and the announcement in July that the 50 acre international services park planned for the Model Farm Road site is to be expanded, with design work beginning immediately, into a 100 acre 'major hi-tech centre . . . with links to the university, the regional college and existing industry' (*The Cork Examiner*, 12 July 1985). The former is being undertaken by the IDA and the latter is a joint venture between the IDA and Cork Corporation.

The policy which would appear to be emerging for these facilities has strong elements drawn from the Business and Technology Centre concept which is placed in a pivotal position in the account of developments in Cork given here. The preparatory work, begun in January, for the Cork Business and Technology Centre is being partly funded by the European Commission. Both the IDA and Cork Corporation are, with others such as the Chamber of Commerce and the University College, members of the sponsoring group for the Business and Technology Centre. While the relationship between these three facilities is a matter of obvious importance which has to be considered by those involved, so as to ensure that the most effective approach possible is devised and without unnecessary cost to the taxpaying public, it has not been possible at this late stage to establish the position as regards their overall relationship and linkages between them and so is not considered at this particular time.

The second qualification which should be briefly stated is that the approach taken here avoids, as consciously as I have been able, any particular ideological attitude in looking at the developments taking place. Much time, thought, and energy goes into debates which, by and large, are conducted in such a manner as to only score debating points and avoid contamination from alternative attitudes. Thus, to state it explicitly, while my personal wish would be for an economic system which was not based on wage-labour and an investment process dependent on incomes being unequally distributed — a characteristic and condition which I regard as part of, and necessary for, a just and peaceful society — the only viewpoint which I have, at least deliberately, admitted and used, I hope, effectively to underpin the study is an entrepreneurial one.

Indeed the *entrepreneurial perspective* (defined in the study) is, I also hope, the only technical, in the sense of jargon, term (but with a precisely defined meaning and context) which has crept into the study. Although the term entrepreneur and its derivative terms are already well on their way to becoming cliches in Ireland, they are, nevertheless, the only terms which I could find to serve my particular needs here. Otherwise, I have made no presumptions as to preferred or feasible forms for organizations or businesses etc.: the problem of entrepreneurship is a problem to be faced by the proponents of all viewpoints struggling to find an answer to the employment problem in a democratic society and a market economy.

And it has to be faced up to by all areas and communities in Ireland, as well as Cork as those of us living here now know only too well.

Finally, it is those people living here who are tackling the challenges we face that have provided the material and approach for this study. It is, in other words, a study by a participating observer grounded on the experience of a particular locality and people rather than being largely, or primarily, based on formal studies and academic literature. Hence, the references to other studies are brief but the debt to persons is extensive and only very inadequately expressed in the acknowledgements.

Connell Fanning,
University College, Cork,
February, 1986

1

Introduction

The collapse of the Verolme Cork Dockyard at the end of 1984 brought Cork near to the bottom of that part of its economic decline which is due to the closure or shrinkage of virtually all the major private enterprises, particularly in goods production, which had been long associated with the area. If the bigger state enterprises whose commercial viability is a matter of concern, especially those in steel, energy, transport, communications, and chemicals, can be made secure in a long-term sense the most severe shocks may be a matter of the past and, even if the bottom has not quite been reached, the process of overall recovery may appear as the more significant feature of the Cork economic situation. The extent and suddenness of the collapse, over a period of about three years, dealt a severe traumatic blow to the sense of confidence and well-being of an entire community whatever the occupation, income, or status of individual members. While the episodes marking decline can be signposted by the demise of the largest employers and some great names associated with Cork it is unlikely, in presently foreseeable circumstances, that many, if any, of the stages in getting off the bottom and rising up again will be so marked. Recovering prosperity will be a slow and difficult process of rebuilding the local economic base in contrast to decline which, as we have learnt, can be shockingly rapid when it gets going.

The most common, and understandable, immediate reaction to what looked at times like an endless series of blows was to regard what was happening in Cork as unique and to call for 'special deals' and 'emergency packages' of government spending as tangible evidence that something was being done. This reaction continued but with less frequency and at an increasingly muted level as it became more apparent that Cork was not the only 'black spot' — there were many before and many to come and, that indeed, all the country was a 'black spot' — so that every twist of the 'special deals game' only served to wind the whole economy further down. It also became increasingly understood that calling for 'packages' of bridges and berths, however high their political visibility as a response to the crisis, only made sense and jobs in the longer-term if there was going to be the commercial activity to ensure the real need for them. As the immediate effects of the shocks to the local economy wore off this new awareness, as reflected in reports and comments in the local news media, emphasised that the energy source for an *entrepreneurial renewal* would have to be local and that creating the right environment — to the extent that it was within the scope of local action — was a prerequisite for releasing it.

The crisis and the new understanding provided by it has already resulted in a number of important actions directing Cork towards becoming an entrepreneurial economy as well as, perhaps most significantly at the outset, initiating a process of changing attitudes. But few of the actions which can be taken locally to promote this fundamental change loom as large or as tangible in public comment, daily perceptions, and political lobbying as bridges and roads. There is, consequently, a danger in assessing the overall response to the crisis to see these developments — which are the most essential in the long-term — as less than they really are because they are taken individually and not placed in a proper relationship with each other. Just as it is necessary to make sense, for example, of a piece of roadway to place it in the overall context of the land use and transportation plan, so too is it necessary to place these other developments in the context of an 'entrepreneurial plan' for the area.

2

The Employment Crisis

A SPECIAL CASE?

During the three years up to the end of 1984, as the economic and social situation worsened, Cork was increasingly characterized as a 'black spot' and a 'special case'. Sometimes a factor held to be specific to Cork was suggested by references to the earlier periods of prosperity and the great 'merchant families' which suggested that a type of economic arterioschlerosis had set in with the consequence that Cork was now slow in moving with the times. This at least pointed to a fundamental fact of economic life: regions and countries can decline as well as develop; change is unavoidable so it is necessary to adapt to retain prosperity. The solutions proposed on the basis of this viewpoint alternated between a 'special deal' and what amounted to giving the 'patient' a good 'shaking-up'.

Even at this stage of the public debate neither diagnosis nor prescription provided the persuasive focus to galvanize a community into action. Perhaps it was because all this was done without supporting evidence or argument, other than the latest twist of the official unemployment register or the most recently announced factory closure, which would have pointed to operational proposals.[1] But, perhaps, it was because they were both based on an assumption which, although usually left implicit, did not ring

---

[1] For one, very belated, attempt by this author to provide some analytical foundations for policy see 'Cork: Towards an Entrepreneurial Economy?' (Paper read to Commission of the European Communities Conference on Innovation and Enterprise, University College, Cork, September 1984.) This, however, pushed the issue substantially beyond the local level to be a matter of national concern to get the overall policy environment right.

true. That assumption was that Cork really was an unemployment 'black spot' relative to the rest of the country during this period. It is necessary to examine that assumption for two reasons. First, it is important for the better design of policy to know if it was valid and, second, if not valid it is important to realise the extent to which scarce resources were wasted and valuable time was lost in the policy debate — if what happened in Cork during that period could be given such a designation. A brief examination of unemployment in the Cork area relative to other areas cast serious doubts on this assumption.[2] The situation as it was in and up to 1983 is set out because it was in the latter half of that year that national attention became focussed on Cork and the public demands for urgent action built up to its highest level.

Starting with the distribution of unemployment by planning regions the numbers registered as unemployed[3] in the South-West, (in which Cork is situated) were 28,743 compared to 69,604 for the East (with Dublin), 16,326 for the Mid-West (Limerick), and 17,261 for the West (Galway) in 1983. In the South-West the growth in absolute terms was from 9,957 in 1960 and 9,434 in 1970 to 12,745 in 1980 and 28,743 in 1983. A similar pattern was observed in other regions.

The rate of unemployment in the South-West was 22·9% compared to a national rate of 20·8%, a Mid-West rate of 24·6%, a West rate of 22·4%, and an East rate of 17·5%. As a share of the national total of unemployment the South-West had 15·2% compared to 36·8% in the East, and 9·1% in the West which had the third largest share. Unemployment in the South-West relative to unemployment in other regions ranged from 41·3% of the East to 265·7% of the North-East.

Thus, the overall impression is that the South-West had *in absolute terms* the second greatest number of unemployed — which, of course, is not surprising since it has the second largest urban concentration of population — but *in relative terms the South-West had fared about the average* and so the region as a whole was not a 'special case'.

For the situation of Cork in particular, the data shows that unemployment in Cork, as a percentage of the national total, was 8·7% in 1960, 7·0% in 1970 and 10·5% in 1983. This again reflected the population concentration in the Cork County Borough. Relative to the South-West plan-

---

2 A more detailed examination is given in Connell M. Fanning, *Cork Towards 800: Crisis and Opportunity,* Doc. XVI/350/84 — EN, Commission of the European Communities, Brussels, June 1984.

3 Unless otherwise noted the data refer to March/April of each year. It should also be noted that lack of area labour force data and the out-of-dateness of available estimates of the national labour force limit the amount of relativity analysis that can be reliably conducted with the live register data.

ning region it had 69·4% of the unemployment in 1983; the Borough part had 36% and the County part had 33·4%. The Cork share had risen by over 13 percentage points since 1960 and the Borough had been affected somewhat worse than the County area.

Within Cork the largest number of unemployed was, of course, in the County Borough which had 10,357 registered unemployed in 1983 compared to a total of 9,598 for the county area; respectively, there were rises from 3,955 and 3,833 in 1980. In 1983 the County Borough had 51·9% of the total and the County had 48·1%. (The second largest concentration of unemployed was registered at the Mallow Office and was only 5·5%). Over the period since 1960 the relative positions of the County and the County Borough have alternated, but generally not very far from each other. The County, in 1983, had about 8 percentage points less than the Borough.

In summary the Borough had by far the greatest number of unemployed in the Cork area and Cork itself significantly the largest proportion of unemployment *within the South-West Region* (which had worsened substantially in recent years) as would be expected from the distribution of population in the region.

Another dimension of the unemployment situation can be seen from the data on percentage of unemployment by duration. The South-West region was generally around the average by duration and gender categories. Percentage long-term unemployment (more than one year) among males had increased in the South-West from 21·8% in 1974 to 35·0% in October 1983. *This was then the lowest rate after the East over all the planning regions.* The same position held for total long-term unemployment. A comparison of the South-West with the rest of the country shows that the unemployment percentages by duration were generally about comparable, with the South-West 7 percentage points lower on the long term unemployment. The actual numbers involved (October 1983) for the South-West ranged from 9,589 long term unemployed (31·4%) down to 2,000-5,000 for the other categories (10%-18%) except for those under 1 week which was 906 (3·0%). Once again within the Cork area the greatest number in all categories were in the County Borough and ranged from 331 for the under-1-week category to 1,000-2,300 for the other categories.

A final dimension for examining how Cork compared to other areas is an examination of youth unemployment (under 25 years) which has received an enormous amount of attention and resources in recent years.[4] In November 1983 the numbers unemployed were 9,450 (17·6% of the

---

[4] This emphasis has been recently questioned by, among others, Brendan M. Walsh, Does Ireland Have a Special Problem of Youth Unemployment?, *Policy Paper No. 10*, Centre for Economic Research, University College, Dublin, February, 1984.

estimated youth labour force) in the South-West and 25,350 (16·4%) in the East. The total was 61,050 and the overall average rate was 16·8%. Thus for unemployment by this age group, *the position once again, in the South-West was much the same as the average for the rest of the country.* The growth rate of total youth unemployment over the period 1980-1984 was 229%, for the South-West it was 255%, and for the East it was 260%. The breakdown for Cork showed that the County Borough had 38·1% of the total South-West youth unemployment, the County had 38·1% and, therefore, overall Cork has again by far the largest proportion, at 76·2% (November 1983), within the South-West which again reflected the concentration of population in Cork areas.

This brief review concentrated on one year to emphasise that *up to 1983 Cork and the South-West, of which Cork is the major part, were not a special problem.* Of course, simply as a matter of timing, there were months when Cork 'looked' relatively worse when the figures were compiled shortly after a large employer shut-down. But after a little while it was the turn of some other area to look worse. As 1984 came and went 'black spots' were 'discovered' all over the country as the relentless increase of unemployment continued. As a result such a designation now carries no weight at all in the public debate and lobbying process and is only a distraction. Looking back at it now it is clear that this should never have been the approach. Time was lost. Talking Cork down — as it amounted to in the end — probably has had other consequences; for example, fewer foreign entrepreneurs are likely to want to go to an area of business decline which obviously devotes its best efforts to politicking and pleading for others, *facing the same problem*, to solve Cork's problem.

The lessons for the future are surely, first, less politicking and instead informed public discussion based on *proper* analysis of accurate information and, then, effective utilization of this for practical purposes which is seriously lacking in Cork; and, second, initiatives based on the robust general impression which emerges from the detailed data that, in relative terms, the South-West or Cork cannot be deemed to have had, nor are likely to have, a relatively more severe overall unemployment problem than other areas. But, of course, in absolute terms the South-West is second only to the East (with Dublin) and, within the South-West, the largest number of unemployed is in the Cork area with the County Borough having the single greatest concentration in these areas and, nationally, the second greatest after Dublin. Therefore, in absolute terms the unemployment situation in Cork, and particularly the Greater Cork Urban Area, is of major concern in the overall Irish context. This together with the importance of the Cork area in the Irish economy, means in turn that Cork cannot be a dependent and lagging region. It must be a net contributor and it should be a leader in the active process of generating higher standards of living and employment in Ireland as a whole. In the following section an indication of the challenge facing Ireland and Cork is presented in order to derive, in Chapter 3, a policy perspective from which the problem may be approached.

EMPLOYMENT REQUIREMENTS

Underlying the present unemployment situation in Cork is (i) a long-term or structural change in the industrial base and employment in Cork as well as (ii) the overall recessionary sitution — due to internal as well as external factors — in the country. Although a 'special case' for Cork, in terms of relative unemployment, would be difficult to sustain there are, nevertheless, aspects of employment and the industrial base which indicate structural factors that merit concern. The changes in employment in the Greater Cork Urban Area is presented in Table 2.1.

Over the period 1971 to 1981 manufacturing showed a very poor growth (less than 0·5%) compared to the national growth rate (12%). Since 1981 manufacturing employment has lost about 1,200 jobs and the closures and cutbacks of recent years have taken away much more than that again. The data in Table 2.2 show the comparative position of the Greater Cork Urban

TABLE 2.1

Employment of Residents of the Greater Cork Urban Area 1971 and 1981

Share (%) in	*1971*	*1981*	*Change*
Agriculture, Mining, Quarrying	3·6	3·0	− 0·6
Manufacturing	18·7	18·8	+ 0·1
Building & Construction	6·2	7·7	+ 1·5
Utilities & Transport	5·6	6·3	+ 0·7
Commerce	13·0	15·2	+ 2·2
Public Administration	3·6	4·6	+ 1·0
Professional Services	7·6	12·4	+ 4·8
Other/Not Stated	4·2	4·9	+ 0·7
TOTAL	62·5	72·8	+10·3
Unemployment	3·1	7·7	+ 4·6
Labour Force	65·6	80·5	+14·9

Source: County Borough Council, Planning Department, from *Census of Population*, 1971 and 1981 (provisional).

TABLE 2.2

Change in Manufacturing Employment in the Greater Cork Urban Area compared to other Urban Areas and National Total, 1973-1983

(January, 1973 = 100)

	GCA	*Limerick*	*Waterford*	*Galway*	*State*
January 1973	100	100	100	100	100
January 1976	95	94	98	134	101
January 1980	103	96	114	183	115
November 1983	86	112	108	170	107

Source: Planning Department, County Borough Council (from IDA Manufacturing Surveys).

Area up to November 1983 and the severe impact of closures up to that date is clearly evident.

From bases of 100 in 1973 Cork has declined to 86 whereas the other urban areas have all expanded manufacturing employment despite the recession (Limerick to 112; Galway to 170, although down from 183 in 1980). A similar pattern in Dublin, despite strong commitments to develop manufacturing, point to particular difficulties in maintaining and expanding the manufacturing base in the larger urban areas. Thus, the recent series of shut-downs in the more traditional manufacturing areas is of concern because the newer manufacturing enterprises are not moving in sufficiently fast to replace the losses.

Professional Services and Commerce were the main sectors contributing to an employment expansion. The Building and Construction industry also had a relatively large increase but this is a sector which is very prone to recessionary impacts and accounts for a high proportion of unemployment. Public Administration grew by 27% during the decade but that was at less than half the overall rate in the state (67%). In general, the expansion of Public Administration was heavily biased towards the eastern half of the country. Manufacturing and Public Administration are the sectors where government influence on location, by incentive or decree, is strongest. Therefore, this, coupled with the fact that in the four years to January 1984 unemployment (live register) grew by 243% in the Greater Cork Area and 204% in Cork County and City compared to 150% in Dublin County and City and 134% nationally, suggests the need to consider the unemployment-employment situation as a combination of structure and politics, rather than a cyclical issue, at least for the Greater Cork Area.

The closure of Dunlops, Fords, and Verolme and, for example, some uncertainty over Irish Steel highlighted the employment crisis during 1983-84. The private firms cited were merely three that were prominent in media accounts but a number of others, without the high profile of these, were and are a cause for concern. Furthermore, the Cork area is now heavily dependent on companies which presently rely as much, if not more, on political/administrative rather than market support for survival and which are in activities where external competitive or administrative factors are important (e.g. oil refining, steel, fertilizers). There are still, therefore, more difficulties and uncertain times ahead on the labour demand side from the existing industrial structure in Cork which has to be faced in devising a strategy for the revitalization of the Cork economy.

There are also difficulties ahead on the labour supply side from the rapid population growth and young age profile that is a dominant feature of the employment challenge in Ireland to-day. Projecting future employment needs is subject to many uncertainties. Any such estimates can only be used as rough indications, within the bounds of the assumptions — fertility rates, migration rates, participation rates — made to calculate them and which have been subject to a high degree of volatility in recent years. For Ireland, estimates suggest that the total labour force could have annual average increases of between *11,000-16,000* persons for the period 1981-1986 and between *16,000-24,000* for the period 1986-1991. The total increase in size of the labour force predicted is 1,318,000-1,342,000 by 1986 and 1,397,000-1,460,000 by 1991. By 1991, nearly 50% of the entire labour force will be in the 25-44 year age category. In 1982 the estimated total employment was 1,146,000 and unemployed was 137,000. The estimated employment needs nationally are in the order of 20,000 net jobs per annum to hold unemployment at an estimated 1986 level of 224,000/240,000 on a live register basis.[5]

Disaggregating labour force projections and estimated employment needs down to local areas compounds further the uncertainties involved. But again in order to indicate the order of magnitude of the task some recent estimates for the Cork area are given in Table 2.3.[6] Table 2.3 shows the net and gross job estimates for Cork County and Cork City on the basis, once again, of a set of assumptions about in and out migration and so on.

To reach a 1989 unemployment rate of 10% the gross job requirements over the period 1984-1989 are 16,020 for Cork County, 9,420 for Cork City, and thus 25,440 in Cork.

Therefore, on the basis of this brief review of the present position and

---

5 Estimates are cited from D. Conniffe and K. Kennedy, editors, *Employment and Unemployment Policy for Ireland*, Economic and Social Research Institute, Dublin, 1984.

6 Planning Department. Employment Needs in Cork. *Mimeo*. Cork County Council, January 1984. The underlying national population base on which these estimates are based differ somewhat from that used in the estimates from the ESRI study providing the estimates for the total labour force and job requirements above.

TABLE 2.3

Estimated Net and Gross Job Requirements 1984-1989 for Cork County and City, given various unemployment rates

Assumed Un-employment Rate (1989)	*Estimated New Jobs Required 1984-1989*			
	Cork County		Cork City	
	NET	GROSS	NET	GROSS
0%	+22,440	+26,610	+13,300	+14,900
5%	+17,140	+21,310	+10,560	+12,160
10%	+11,850	+16,020	+ 7,820	+ 9,420
15%	+ 6,550	+10,720	+ 5,080	+ 6,680
20%	+ 1,260	+ 5,430	+ 2,340	+ 3,940
25%	− 4,040	+ 130	− 400	+ 1,200

Source: Planning Department, Employment Needs in Cork, *Mimeo*, Cork County Council, January 1984.

outlook, the situation in which Cork now finds itself clearly poses a major challenge. But, despite the recent setbacks and the impact of any further ones to come, there are significant resources in Cork on which to build a response for employment. These include, for example,

— substantial port facilities, especially in the light of the Government's decision to finance the deepwater berth at the Ringaskiddy seaport and to provide instrument landing systems at the airport;
— a major natural resource area for the agricultural and tourist industries;
— major gas and potential petroleum energy supplies off the coast;
— substantial third-level educational and research institutions and organizations and manpower training facilities and programmes providing professional, technical, and craft skills for people as well as a significant research base for industry;
— a planned IDA International Services park;
— an already established base in the electronics and micro-electronics industry and a developing modern potential in other science based industries e.g. biotechnology and food biotechnology and food processing, backed up by the expanding local research capabilities.

Thus, while the needs are considerable so are the resources with which to approach them. The challenges facing Cork are also faced by every other part of Ireland. How Ireland fares will therefore depend, perhaps more than ever before, on the local responses in areas such as Cork. To provide a perspective on the direction such responses are taking and should, perhaps, take, a number of policy implications from the analysis so far are presented in the next chapter.

3

A Policy Perspective

One result of the continually increasing level of unemployment in Ireland is that some people are reconsidering the 'concept' of unemployment, very often on the unsupported assertion that the level will always rise or, at least, not decline. They are, therefore, suggesting new approaches to 'live with it'. The new approaches involve 'educating the unemployed for leisure', job-sharing schemes, and so on. Quite apart from the obvious questions of who shall be unemployed? whose job shared? who will provide the support? and at what level?, there are the basic questions of who will decide who will 'enjoy leisure'? and how will it be decided and enforced?

Obviously the present period is one of rapid change with adaptive mechanisms appearing to be quite slow. Yet, on the longer term view there is no logical or, so far, definitive empirical reason to hold that unemployment must rise inexorably and that the goal of a high employment economy has to be jettisoned. Thus, while policies are needed to alleviate the undesirable effects of adjustment, they should not be based on the presumption that major change is not occurring now, will not continue to occur, or can be ignored and disguised. In other words, the reality of change and the need for continuing adaptation must be recognized.

Although quite widely accepted — if somewhat fatalistically at times — by the general public there is not yet an open admission by political representatives or a government that the unemployment crisis is not primarily a cyclical phenomenon in Ireland and will not be resolved by any plausible up-turn in world trade. The world recession combined with the public debt crisis has forced out, earlier than would otherwise have been the case, the inherent weakness of Irish economic development policy, i.e.

the lack of a coherent entrepreneurial policy. The present position is an ill-assorted mix of viewpoints, policies, instruments, and proposals struggling for action.

A central concern in the present debate about employment policy centres around the question: will *the* jobs come from the private or the public sector? One view holds that the private sector cannot create enough jobs to meet the employment needs of the future and, furthermore, that it has never done so in the past. Sometimes this is said simply as a statement of fact and, at other times, as a prelude to the additional view that the private sector has, therefore, 'failed' in Ireland. The implication drawn — and often taken to be apparently obvious — is that the answer to the employment crisis must, therefore, lie with the state sector. However, as often as not, what is meant by the 'state sector' — administrative or commercial, centralized or decentralized — is left vague as is also the full content of the 'private sector' designation. The latter is even left vague by the proponents of the view that it is the private sector where the future for employment lies. The rallying points in this case are the elliptical aspherisms that the government cannot create wealth and (many/most) 'state sector' jobs are unproductive. Rarely does the — again apparently obvious — policy stance actually involve a *private* sector answer but, almost invariably, a different and preferred assortment of state interventions to promote particular private interests.

The obvious point which tends to be ignored is that neither the 'private' *nor* the 'public' sector have failed simply because neither *one* has been tried. It has always been a mixture and it cannot be presumed that the particular mixtures were the best ones to achieve high employment; despite the public rhetoric they weren't mixtures created specifically, or even primarily, to do so. And if the criterion of success or failure is the generation of sufficient jobs, so as to result in a low unemployment rate plus emigration rate, the simple fact is that the entire economy of the Republic has 'failed', since independence at least, to meet the employment needs. To characterise the outcome for the whole economy as a 'failure' ignores the fact that a very large number of jobs were actually generated in *both* the private and public sectors. These were faced, however, with the great needs resulting from the decline in traditional industries — agricultural and non-agricultural — as well as from labour force expansion so that overall the net addition to employment was almost always inadequate.

It could be said with validity that the private sector jobs were only created with the aid of expensive state sector support schemes. The obvious retort is that the tax revenues to finance not only those schemes but much of the state sector contribution to employment came from the private sector. And, in principle at least, that is true. However, it is also true that a very large amount of actual state financing for both sectors came from borrowed money — much of it foreign — to such an extent that the process was unsustainable. The argument that the private sector has failed or, more mildly, that it cannot meet the jobs needs of the country and consequently that the employment must be provided in the state sector, although tax-financed, begs the question as to whether sufficient jobs would or could survive in the private or, more broadly, commercial net-tax-paying sector with the levels of taxation which would be involved in providing the finance for employment on the necessary scale. The dilemma is not an easy one to resolve. But, perhaps, looking at it in terms of either/or, as is the case with much political debate, is not the best way. It is more likely to be a matter of the private sector *with* the public sector except that new relationships and appropriate organizations must be discovered to supplement or replace existing ones. Unfortunately, while some developments are already taking place, the political will or implementation skills appear to be inadequate when measured against the total challenge.

The fundamental perspective which must orientate thinking about these problems is a very simple one and precedes any argument about 'public versus private': when an economy is undergoing structural change or economic transition *the most critical factor, tautologically, is entrepreneurship*, i.e. the alertness to 'see' profitable opportunities and the willingness to act in response to them, coupled with the necessary conditions — incentives and scope — to search out and act upon opportunities perceived. No matter what aids are employed, in the end, only human beings can do this; so it obviously requires people to be entrepreneurs. The essential role of entrepreneurship as an active factor of change, and entrepreneurs as agents of change, has long been recognised. Correspondingly, although perhaps less often recognised, the most effective organizational unit of entrepreneurial change in a market economy is the business firm. Neither have been given that practical recognition which is essential for a dynamic economy in Ireland.

Ireland has relied heavily on foreign sources for entrepreneurship in 'modern' competitive lines of activity. The competition for this, and the industrial projects game which distributes catches internally, has been instrumental in shaping not only industrial policy but also entrepreneurial policy such as it is. Although relatively successful, the competition among countries for internationally mobile enterprise is now very strong. As well as this there are aspects, e.g. the repatriation of large profits taken in Ireland for tax relief through distortionary transfer pricing mechanisms, which although they may still be needed, further limit the reliance that can be placed on this source. As a result there has been increasingly widespread agreement that the greatest reliance has to be placed on indigenous and, obviously, locally based enterprises. But the employment needs of Ireland are on such a scale that it appears inevitable that previous approaches to 'creating jobs' and, more broadly, present overall industrial policy will not be adequate. (Indeed it is difficult to imagine any administrative approach, other than perhaps the establishment of a fully centrally administered economy, if that were feasible in Ireland, which is likely to match these requirements; and this would have to do so in a highly controlled and regimented way.) The response to the employment challenge will have to be on a much more widespread and fundamental level. Given the environment in which Ireland must survive, there is not sufficient financial, entrepreneurial, and managerial capability in the country for the dominant approach at present to succeed in generating a high employment society, except in that mythical country, 'political promisedland', which enjoys a peculiar reality in Ireland.

The resolution of the employment problem will have to involve the entire labour force and population in an active way rather than in the present, predominantly passive, way of waiting to be hired or for the 'government to create jobs'. Unfortunately, to the extent that there is an active popular response it is to seek political rather than economic 'solutions' even if these are frequently conducted under the guise of setting up *enterprises* and *creating employment*. (Much too often profits appear to be virtually synonymous with state agency grants, i.e. enforced — by taxation — transfers from one group to another.) But these cannot be real solutions in the sense that the problem is removed — it has usually only been transferred to someone or somewhere else.

In other words the process of founding and running modern, competitive enterprises will have to be spread wider throughout the population — in a phrase the task ahead is to *democratize entrepreneurship*. And what does democratizing entrepreneurship mean? It means, on the one hand, that barriers and obstacles to entrepreneurial action must go and, on the other hand, that some mechanisms must be developed by which people can get into business, if necessary on a small firm scale, i.e. have access to capital and have an incentive to do so. One incentive is obviously money. Another is the pressure for employment. Furthermore, the pattern of recruitment from among the unemployed, e.g. the recruitment pattern for grant-aided industry in Ireland in 1979 showed only 18·4% coming from the Live Register of Unemployed (Table 3.1) and suggests specifically the urgent need to direct active and substantial attention at promoting entrepreneurship and enterprise creation among currently unemployed persons. In interpreting this data allowance must be made for the low rate of unemployment which appeared to hold in 1979. This was estimated as 6·9% according to the Labour Force Survey and 9·9% according to the Live Register procedures. (This is the only year for which such data is available.)

This focus on entrepreneurship raises an important question about the quantity and distribution of entrepreneurial capability in Ireland. The persistence of the employment problem indicates that adaptiveness to economic changes is slow and points to entrepreneurship as one significantly limiting resource. Does Ireland lack entrepreneurial capability? In other words, do we lack the necessary characteristics to exploit our entrepreneurial potential, namely,

— abilities (practical training, mental training, and 'habits of mind')
— attitudes (desire, willingness, and will for the effort and risk)
— rewards (financial and non-financial)
— resources (e.g. in principal only a 'good idea' is necessary but in practice personal finance is also required to create a business)?

Entrepreneurship seems to thrive in all sorts of environments and climates. But at this stage we can only point out — and sometimes only very tentatively — what *inhibits* it rather than say what *will* produce it. Like art it appears to be impossible to produce the process or arrange the outcome artificially. However it is essential to bear in mind that we simply don't know the answers to many of the issues raised by these questions and it would be unwise to pretend or presume we do.

But, while these are very difficult areas to assess, there are causes for concern about the narrow distribution of entrepreneurial capability among our population. These include:

1. At home and abroad the Irish would appear to have demonstrated enough entrepreneurial capability to, at least, question any racial basis for limitations. But the long drain of actual and potential entrepreneurs may have seriously depleted the domestically resident pool of entrepreneurial potential. An increasing rate of emigration of skilled

TABLE 3.1

Recruitment Pattern for Grant-Aided Industry in Ireland 1979*

Source of Labour	*School Leavers & AnCO Trainees*	*Live Register*	*Manufacturing*	*Agri culture (Transfers)*	*Other*	*Returned Emigrants*	*Housewives*	*Total*
%	23·3	18·4	24·1	4·9	17·0	3·6	8·7	100
Numbers	4,450	3,515	4,603	936	3,247	688	1,622	19,000

Source: John McKeon, Economic Analysis of Industrial Projects in Ireland, *Journal of the Statistical and Social Inquiry Society of Ireland* XXIV (2), 1979/80 p. 126, Table 1. Original source cited is *Industrial Development Authority, Survey of Recruitment Patterns,* I.D.A., Dublin 1980.

* Date not explicitly identified in text; content suggests 1979.

and business persons and the establishment of foreign bases by a very high proportion of the larger firms add further to the concern.

2. An educational system which, it is widely believed, does not promote the values of creative and innovative thinking or encourage the individual initiative that are essential for entrepreneurship. (Whatever merit 'games' may have the answer to this, if valid, is more fundamental than 'playing at business' as a sideline to the regular education process.)
3. Different ways of organising for businesses affect the realization of the entrepreneurial potentialities of employees who constitute the largest part of the working population. Despite some enlightened exceptions among management, the basic interest of hierarchical capitalist organizations tends to dominate. People are hired as workers to follow standard procedures as much as possible and thus are not required or wanted to show initiative or insight into their work or into the business since it might undermine management or trade union prerogatives. Possibly the trade union dilemma will be of greater importance in the future as the involvement of employees may increase.
4. Entrepreneurs do not emerge from any one particular social class or income group. Although, if successful they may gravitate in terms of lifestyles towards a particular social group, e.g. the 'middle class' etc., the source of entrepreneurs is not confined to this group. Nor is it a talent which is inherited within any single social class or family, as is shown often by the failure of later generations to successfully run a business. But the complexities of getting into and doing business in Ireland probably acts as a barrier to many persons less educated and skilled in handling these demands and less confident about taking them on.
5. Irish policy towards business and entrepreneurship has tended more and more towards administrative rather than market approaches to business. Some elements in the recent *White Paper on Industrial Policy*[1] appear to take developments a stage further along administrative lines. Perhaps this is all a consequence of the complexities of business. It may also be a short-run response to a narrow entrepreneurial base and an attempt to make the little we have go as far as possible. But it doesn't directly address the fundamental problems possibly because many of the relevant factors are deemed to be outside the scope of the industrial policy 'pigeon-hole' in the structures of public administration and government organization.

Overall the persistence of the employment problem coupled with the

---

[1] Ireland, *White Paper on Industrial Policy*, P1. 2491 Stationary Office, Dublin, July 1984.

previous and continuing drain of actual and potential entrepreneurs would suggest the need to address entrepreneurial capability as a key limiting resource. The long-term issue is a major improvement in the entrepreneurship resources of the country; in the short-term it means the development of existing firms and increasing the rate of firm formation on the basis of existing entrepreneurial resources. Expansion of entrepreneurial potential and improvement in the realization of that potential is a difficult task and attempts to discover effective approaches need to follow some general guidelines.

First, and foremost, the need is for entrepreneurs. It is at the smaller end of the enterprise size scale that new entrepreneurs tend to be generated. People who work in small business are more likely to start a business than those working in large enterprises because, among other reasons, it appears to be important to see all the operations in a business.[2] (This latter aspect is also relevant for people who, on being made redundant from large enterprises, have the initiative and ability to respond by starting their own firms.) Special attention should be paid to new and growing businesses at the small end of the scale. But this does not imply that small firms are the direct answer to the unemployment problem and that all we need is a few more. The focus on such firms arises from the need for (i) an entrepreneurial approach, (ii) for any approach to be based on indigenous enterprise, and (iii) relationships between small firms or, more generally, small scale decentralized units of larger enterprise and entrepreneurship and innovativeness. The explicit concern in Ireland must be with small firms with a potential for growth and the realization of that potential. Only in that way can small firms be a key element in the creation of wealth and employment on the scale which is needed in Ireland.

Second, the scale and apparent permanency of the employment problem has brought about the realization that (i) a domestic enterprise approach is the only plausible one which can be followed to restore high employment; (ii) it must be based on local communities; and (iii) has to address the problem of entrepreneurship and business initiative among unemployed persons generally. The first aspect is now well established, officially as well as unofficially, and the process of devising appropriate instruments has begun already. But, as yet, informal recognition of the latter two aspects is well ahead of formal adjustment and the discovery and development of suitable responses is only at a very preliminary stage in Ireland.

Once it is recognised that foreign capital and entrepreneurship cannot form the core of our approach — however valuable it may be as a suppor-

---

[2] Martin Binks and John Coyne, *The Birth of Enterprise: An Analytical and Empirical Study of the Growth of Small Firms,* Hobart Paper 98, Institute of Economic Affairs, London, 1983.

ting instrument — and once 'indigenous' enterprise becomes the matter of central concern it quickly follows that the arena for action is the local community and the task is, therefore, to devise strategies and methods of implementation which create local environments conducive to enterprise formation and expansion. In that context unemployment has become a matter for local economic initiatives, rather than a part of the national political 'competition for jobs'.

There is no question, obviously, that politics and administration at the national level play an essential role in making the overall, i.e. national, environment in which local communities must pursue their resolution of this problem. While it is also necessary to address the national environment, where much has to be done, the usual type of response which follows from a local political outcry rarely addresses the real entrepreneurial needs of a community. Even if the occasional foreign industrial project is directed to mask the latest 'black spot' somewhere it is, on balance, a 'no-winner' game. Specifically, if Cork wants foreign enterprises, the most effective way to assist in the worldwide competition for them is as a dynamic business area — a community with a vibrant sense of entrepreneurship will attract far more foreign capital than its opposite with any amount of political to-and-fro. Paradoxically, some short-term gains of foreign enterprises may result in long-term losses as the feedback about local conditions increases knowledge among foreign investors.

Third, once the domestic enterprise and local initiative implications are recognised the necessary approaches will have to be developed *from* and *for* the Irish and local situation. There are no simple, readily available answers for Ireland or Cork and, while we can learn from the best *relevant* attempts in other countries, we cannot import a solution. It will have to be found by a process of discovery which grapples with the particular jumble of problems and resources that emerges from the national and local combinations of political, social, and economic factors. The overall mix is crucial and we shall have to think it out for ourselves both at national and local levels, and not look to the latest unimaginative unemployment support scheme or tax concession for investment emanating, for example, from London which derive from a sufficiently different political, social, and economic history as to warrant a more critical public appraisal than has been usual. Perhaps a policy of innovation first and then looking around to compare might do better; if we cannot innovate in terms of internal economic and social arrangements how can we expect to be able to innovate product and process technology in competition with the fast runners in the race we must run?

Fourth, the reasoning that the resolution of the local, and hence national, employment problems will only come if based *on* (but not exclusively *from*) local entrepreneurship does not naively imply that everyone will or must be a great entrepreneur. Just as the number of people who 'really matter' in any firm or organization — even the largest — is a tiny proportion of the total so, too, the number of entrepreneurs that will 'matter' will be quite small.

As yet such entrepreneurs cannot be arranged; it is not, and is unlikely ever to be, a case of selecting specific babies, children, etc. and 'incubating' them to become great entrepreneurs. To get enough of them to meet the needs of local areas and the country as a whole requires an environment that is conducive to *entrepreneurship in general.* It is in getting the overall environment as right as we know how for entrepreneurs, and not in stage-managing the various 'ages of *entrepreneurial* man', that resources and effort would appear to be best directed.

At the same time, while it is clear that entrepreneurs cannot be arranged, neither need there be a great mystery about it. There are hundreds of thousands of entrepreneurs in Ireland. For example, farmers and small shopkeepers alone constitute a significant proportion of the population. Thus, *the basic premise which underlies an argument for local initiatives* is that the distribution of entrepreneurial potential, like any human talent, is equally distributed across appropriately large populations and that what distinguishes communities and areas in terms of entrepreneurship are the obstacles to the realization of that potential in the community. In the absence of convincing evidence to the contrary this premise points to the necessity of, as well as providing the working basis for, community based entrepreneurial initiatives. The problem is that the potential is not being realized to a sufficient extent and in directions suitable for meeting the employment needs of each community.

Fifth, and finally, once the emphasis is on indigenous enterprise and local initiatives, an issue which needs to be briefly mentioned concerns what enterprises and lines of activity should be promoted and facilitated in an entrepreneurial approach to employment generation. Firms must be trade competitive as Ireland is primarily a trading nation. From where will these firms come? A prominent theme in current policy thinking suggests a 'selectivist' approach — the identification of 'key' firms in 'key' internationally *traded* activities. 'Selectivism' raises many questions, e.g. the problems of 'picking winners' in the first place and keeping these winners in the second place, which cannot be dealt with here. But the difficulties of competitiveness are substantial and not to be under-estimated if that is to be the primary approach.[3] If industrial policy is about competitiveness in

---

3 'Selectivism' differs significantly from the approach pursued until recently, of attracting major foreign enterprises because that is primarily a matter of persuading previously identified 'winners' to locate some part of their production facilities in Ireland.

the end, it is about competitiveness at the outset, and if the goal is market competitiveness, then the market must ultimately be the selection process so the design of policy and instruments for its implementation must recognize the inherent logic of market systems.

Basically, since Ireland has no option but to be a competitive trading economy *all sectors*, however they are categorized — 'exposed' or 'sheltered', trading or non-trading — must contribute to continually improving the competitive position. There is a view, drawn, for example, from U.S. experience, that 'the jobs' will be in services rather than manufacturing because of slower productivity growth and the 'sheltered' nature of services. But much of services in Ireland are open to foreign competition; tourism, for example, is very largely a part of foreign trade in Ireland; neither is the categorization of local newspapers as non-traded goods sensible or helpful if readers substitute national for local papers and if national papers are replaced by foreign papers as is the case in Ireland. Added to this is the fact that many non-traded sectors are *directly* inputs to costs but also, in terms of standard-of-living effects on wage demands, are all *indirectly* inputs to costs of the 'exposed' foreign trading category of enterprises, making it pointless to be so categorical for industrial and entrepreneurial policy purposes.

Furthermore, if the issue is one of entrepreneurship then all the non-foreign trading sectors are crucial determinants of the overall entrepreneurial environment and, furthermore, could be the source of entrepreneurial teams which are a crucial factor for enterprise creation and development.

Policy should not be based on categorization schemes or numbers which are convenient to administrators or economists and, whatever about the implications for national policy (which is not directly of concern here), certainly local initiatives should not be tied to narrow constraints for entrepreneurship promotion and business formation and expansion.[4] Employment-orientated local initiatives based on promoting and facilitating entrepreneurship in all lines of activity and for all types of firms will have to discover new instruments and arrangements among existing instruments which are suitable to meet the peculiarities of each area.

In the next chapter the general requirements for enterprise creation and

---

[4] Arguments for 'selectivism' are given from a corporatist viewpoint, i.e. society seen as an organization which can be centrally directed by the key business, government, and trade union managers who 'create a consensus' by Leonard Wrigley, 'Ireland in Economic Space' (in J. Lee, editor, *Ireland Towards a Sense of Place*, Cork University Press, Cork, 1985) and 'Towards the Next 1,000 Issues' (*Business and Finance:* 9-11, 17 May 1984); and from a socialist viewpoint, with emphasis on the role of the state and its agencies, by Eoin O'Malley, 'Industrial Development Strategy in Ireland: A Left Perspective' (*Mimeo*, January 1983).

expansion at the small end of the size-scale are outlined and the resources available locally in Cork for assisting and facilitating this process of enterprise formation and expansion are then reviewed. This then provides the basis for identifying the issues which have to be faced in devising a local entrepreneurial-based strategy for employment and suggesting the type of responses which may be appropriate. This is done in Chapter 5 which, in turn, provides the background against which the emerging local response to the crisis emerging in Cork can be delineated in Chapter 6. Together these also provide a perspective for evaluating the relevance of the response to crisis and approach to renewing the local economy emerging in Cork to other areas.

4

Requirements and Resources for Enterprise Creation and Development

REQUIREMENTS FOR START-UP AND EXPANSION

The requirements for creating a new enterprise and developing a going business concern can be broadly grouped under three headings:

— People and Organization
— Finance and Premises
— Marketing and Technology

People and Organization

The first requirement — and always the single most important one — in business activity is entrepreneurship and the people, organizations and an environment conducive to it. *Entrepreneurship* is a term used loosely to cover the elements essential for business: perception of opportunity under uncertainty, setting clear goals and the will to act on them; vision and commitment; and leadership and organizational qualities to achieve tasks set for the enterprise. The factors underlying the supply and quality of entrepreneurship are varied and complex and include, for example, educational and social aspects, motivation and incentive frameworks (e.g. desire for independence and control as well as monetary return), and general economic and social environments (degree of uncertainty and instability, appreciation for role of entrepreneur in the community etc.).

The successful conduct of entrepreneurship involved the right combination of people and organization whatever the size of the enterprise. But the size of the business organization is an important variable in how it can survive and develop in the context of continually changing market environments.

Most of the same basic functions have to be carried out in small firms just as in large firms, but the organizational capability and structures are quite different. In the smaller firms the operation of a business is conducted largely on a personal basis. As a firm grows it must move towards operating on the basis of policies and formal organization. This requires changing the firm and, therefore, investment in the broadest economic sense. A larger business cannot always be run the same way that a small business can be 'kept going' or even successful because the larger size requires different approaches and attitudes which have to be learnt and set up. As the scale of operation expands the changes which usually become unavoidable include:

(i) management becoming a full-time activity for at least one person;
(ii) one individual no longer able to set the objectives for the enterprise;
(iii) technical specialists may be necessary; and
(iv) organizational, including legal, changes in structure may be desirable or unavoidable.

As a corollary to the essential requirement for *an* entrepreneur in any business there is the need to develop an *entrepreneurial team*. But a new or small enterprise has very limited resources — and, indeed, sometimes even only promises — with which to do that. Small businesses generally do not provide the environment for development of management and organization which may be a pre-requisite, or at least a concomitant, of expansion and survival. They are not noted for good internal relations, communications, and organization of tasks and responsibilities. And they are also severely limited in their resources to support the management and investment in the overall change which they need. The unwillingness or failure to see the need and to organize for analysis and planning of growth and change will very often result in bottlenecks to expansion which, even if overcome, may leave the firm permanently weakened or achieving less than its full potential. It is therefore necessary that new and existing small firms acquire, or have access to, the planning capability crucial to developing a larger business if the potential is there. This means that the inadequate development of team work and technical capabilities, delegation of decision-making, and management structure and organizational development which characterizes many small firms must be overcome. It also means that the poor industrial relations which are not uncommon, should be addressed in the overall interests of a good, sound business. The means by which these can be achieved include:

- the arrangement of processes and organization for analysis, planning, decision-making and evaluation of the whole enterprise;
- the orientation of top management less towards day-to-day activities and more towards the future and objectives of the enterprise;
- the development of a board of directors to bring an external and in-

formed perspective to bear on the business and, most importantly, to see the business as a whole and devise its strategy;
- the selection and training of new and existing personnel for a larger scale operation; and
- arranging the employment policy of the firm.

Finance and Premises

The three main types of finance for a firm are equity, loans, and grants. The sources for these and their relative importance vary depending on the type and size of a business and the line of activity pursued. For instance, and with a few exceptions (including some tourism,) virtually all of service activities may be excluded from the main state grants for industrial development as is the case in Ireland. Restrictions may also apply to incentives available for other types of finance for business activities.

But there is also a significant difference in the sources of finance between new and existing ventures due to the simple fact that, by definition, new firms do not have a historical record of profitability and hence credit-worthiness. Thus, in the establishment of a new business, personal funds may be the most important, if not the only, source of equity funding. This along with state grants, in one form or another, may provide the largest proportion of seed capital for the start-up financial package. This means that the ability to save, as well as raise personally guaranteed loans, and the reward incentive to do so are an important influence on firm formation and the initial capitalisation of new firms. They are not only a source of finance but are also an indication to other lenders of commitment by an entrepreneur to the project.[1]

The other main sources of founding capital are usually not open to new small firms. The stock market is not, as presently arranged, a financing institution which meets the needs of small scale capital borrowers. A new, small firm cannot readily issue marketable equity shares. An entrepreneur requiring capitalization, say, at £10,000-£20,000 cannot go to the stock market because, for relatively small amounts it would cost more than the capital being sought to raise it on the stock exchange. Unless the capital of a firm is, at least, about £2·5m it does not pay to make a public issue at present in Ireland.

Similarly, venture capital fund institutions and partnerships are faced with relatively high costs involved in evaluating investment proposals and for continuing management assistance or participation. They are therefore usually geared towards financing the development of established firms — or, at least, entrepreneurs — with potential for large-scale development.

---

[1] Frequently in practice, however, the *commitment of personal funds*, to qualify for state grants, may also actually include the *retention* of future *projected* profits!

They do not usually provide finance for small firms. Also entrepreneurs are quite often unwilling to surrender a relatively high proportion of the equity of their firm for relatively little capital investment. There is a dislike of surrendering control as they put themselves in the position of having already sold a significant part of their firm when they later seek funds for expansion, which could result in loss of control entirely by the original promoter, or seek to sell out entirely to realize the value of their efforts.

The costs and difficulties involved in evaluating small business loans also affects the ability and willingness of commercial banks to fund new and small-scale ventures. The time and expense involved in making a small loan could be as great as for a large loan. Such firms do not have a record of past profitability — and hence a basis for projecting future profitability — or sufficient value of realisable assets which determine creditworthiness for loans. A limited, or complete lack of a, business history means that projections of profitability are discounted by a high risk factor. Furthermore, branch managers of large banks may not have the expertise or resources at their disposal for identifying survival and growth prospects of firms. Since risk and security are ultimately matters of understanding and judgement, there is then a tendency to require personal guarantees for business loans — which are sometimes over-secured — so that the benefits of limited liability for an entrepreneur are virtually eliminated. The overall result can be a bias towards larger scale operations and towards making judgements on the basis of social or educational factors rather than the merits of a particular small venture and particular entrepreneur.

On the other side of the funding problem is the fact that very often difficulties in obtaining finance may be due to the lack of necessary entrepreneurial capability or capital raising ingenuity. The entrepreneur with a dedication to product or customer may not be able to convey the necessary sense of confidence to potential lenders. It again brings to the centre of attention the need for an entrepreneurial team because the one or two entrepreneurs usually founding a small business may not have all the necessary capabilities. And they are even more unlikely to have all these necessary for the development of an enterprise. In particular poor financial management, especially, of cash flow and short-term liquidity, are common features of small firms. Of the firms that *fail* the largest proportion tends to be firms in the first five or so years of their existence. Inefficient cash management and capital productivity, resulting in inadequate liquidity, are significant contributing factors, especially in the case of smaller firms. Therefore, perhaps as serious as the actual shortage of funds is the shortage or inadequacy of personnel with the necessary skills both at the outset and for the development of a firm. These problems have to be addressed in any firm so that potential lenders, especially banks which are critical, are satisfied with the credit risk of the business.

Although their nature may change, financing difficulties, nevertheless, continue to be a major factor in the development of a business. A firm intending to expand must anticipate the financial structure and identify the financial resources it will need two or more years ahead, depending on the investment involved and particular as well as general aspects of the firms environment, and proceed to make arrangements well in advance to get the best terms.

Growth and development require investment which requires that a business be controlled carefully for its cash flow in order to avoid liquidity crises, and disturbance to lender confidence, that can hamper growth and reduce future potential for development.

Usually by the time an expansion is to be undertaken all personal funds have already been committed and external sources must be tapped. Furthermore, the financing needs of different parts of the business grow differently and overall do not grow proportionately with sales volume. Also smaller firms may require relatively greater amounts of finance to expand their capital base than larger firms. The development phase, which is one of greatest growth potential, is one where the ability to raise funds is often severely limited and at the same time survival requires expansion. It is also at this stage that many other factors affect the financing position of the firm, e.g. taxation and labour costs, and may differentially affect a larger firm, and hence one trying to become larger, than a smaller one. Such factors often give rise to firms with growth potential staying small for convenience or to stay hidden in the 'black economy'.

A particularly important aspect of the finance problem is the need for suitable premises for the business. Although this aspect has received much attention for manufacturing and some service activities it is nevertheless one that can still cause difficulties, in particular, for those excluded from certain types of state aided or provided facilities. It is also necessary that the arrangement of premises be flexible to accommodate the expanding — and contracting — needs of a business with the minimum disruption. At the outset, and later for development, the options of leasing or purchasing existing or purpose-built premises has to be considered from the viewpoints of operation and financing and very often firms are constrained in the options available or by commitments previously entered into under different circumstances.

Marketing and Technology

As with most other important functions the small firm must overcome marketing problems although it may not have the personnel or resources to tackle them in the same way as in a larger firm. Directly or indirectly someone in the firm or associated with the firm must fulfill the marketing function. At least as much, if not more so, the causes of failure among new and small firms has to do with basic management and marketing planning (including sales) ability as they have to do with size, financial shortage, and, perhaps, even product quality and skills.

The firm, to develop, must pay a great deal of attention to markets, products, and technologies. Small firms find it difficult to keep up to date with ideas, markets, technologies, personnel, and skills. Products may not be adapted or developed rapidly enough — if at all — to changing market conditions and opportunities. Poor marketing — often no more than trying to sell what has been already produced — and poor service to customers are common features among small firms. This is particularly serious in Ireland because, due to the small size of the home market, small firms are forced to seek foreign markets at an earlier stage of their development than their counterparts in bigger economies.

Planning is essential and the personnel and organization to do so a basic requirement. Product and market expansion has to be financed and it is necessary to have some product at a stage of generating positive net revenues to do so. The development of an entrepreneurial team and organization is once again a central matter since strategic decisions have to be made about the markets, products and technologies which will be the objective of the firm. Growth requires information; so future information requirements have to be anticipated and effective means of collection and evaluation organized. An investment programme in marketing, production, and organizational capabilities has to be devised, implemented and financed. All these put severe strains on the resources of new and small firms but, handled ineffectively, can result in bottlenecks to actual growth and limit the potential, as well as the realization of potential, of the business.

There is, however, another dimension which is separate from, but interacts with, the effects of small scale enterprises. This is the regional dimension to technology which, in the case of the Irish economy, also involves the smallness and regionality of the whole economy. The fundamental reality of such a situation is that any small economy must import most of its basic science and technology as well as raw materials. And if basic research and, indeed, actual innovation occur elsewhere the speed at which information and knowledge can be transferred and commercially operationalized, i.e. supply got to the market, is crucial to the innovative capability — and hence competitiveness — of a regional economy. But small indigenous firms in a regional economy do not usually have the resources, especially personnel with technical competence, or even the attitude, to *individually* be effective channels for innovation. Evidence suggests that firms in regional-policy-assisted and less developed regions are slower to adopt innovations than firms in non-assisted regions.[2] Grants,

[2] J.B. Goddard, A.T. Thwaites, and D.C. Gibbs, 'Technological Change and Regional Development', paper delivered to ESRC/CURDS Workshop on

while they may act as an incentive initially, may also act to blunt the keenness which is essential for competitiveness by softening the commercial pressure on firms.

The key functions to be performed are, first, the sourcing of ideas and know-how and, second, the planning, decision-making, marketing, technical design and development, and production processes to exploit the opportunity identified. New and small firms in less developed areas tend to be inadequate on both counts and meeting these requirements tend to be beyond the immediate financial, manpower, and organizational capability of these firms. Since small autonomous firms are assumed to be adaptable this implies that for a *region* to be innovative small firms *as a group* must play the role that is held for them individually *in theory*. In other words, the costs of innovation must be shared and their capabilities increased by (somehow) pooling the overhead functions which are beyond the resources and capabilities of such firms individually.

But it is not just a matter of the degree of dynamism and extent of resources of small firms even as a group. The innovativeness of small firms depends to a very great extent on their regional environment. In particular it depends on the degree of integration of these firms into innovation networks and the capability of the regional financing institutions to evaluate innovative business proposals. For example, the information gap usually extends to the financial institutions link in the 'chain of innovation' by small firms. Banks in less developed areas do not usually have the personnel capable of accurately evaluating *apparently* high-risk propositions. The distance factor to more metropolitan centres, where such expertise resides, is an important barrier to those institutions financing somewhat remote and unknown entrepreneurs.

On the basis of this brief consideration we see that the requirements for innovation in a regional economy — and the instrument for an innovation-orientated regional strategy — include:

(i) business resources focussed on utilization and adaptation of known technologies rather than on basic research;
(ii) concentration on take-up by firms of innovation, i.e. their attitude and capability to search, arrange, and utilize new technologies;
(iii) the ability to do so as effectively and as early as possible by adequate integration into the diffusion process and innovation networks;
(iv) financial institutions capable of adapting to new entrepreneurial demands.

The emphasis is, therefore, on the channels and instruments of information transfer and the operationalization of knowledge obtained, i.e.

Technological Change, Industrial Restructuring and Regional Development, University of Newcastle, March 1984.

application, production, and marketing. In these areas the state agencies and institutions — national and local — can be significant elements in the facilities appropriate to each. The crucial factor in advisory systems are the implementation procedures rather than the geographical location of 'national' facilities. There are a number of further requirements emerging from the analysis which have to be met by the state agencies to increase the capability of local firms to utilize innovations and ensure a more even distribution of innovativeness;

(i) the advisory agencies need to be effectively tied into the process of innovation, i.e. commercial application of research and invention, by instruments which ensures responsibility and accountability;
(ii) since specific opportunities and needs cannot be known in advance the procedures must also be flexible and responsive;
(iii) the assistance has to be delivered in a manner that recognises that innovation by a firm affects internal relations and raises sensitive issues and so does not also run into the objection of too much government or 'bureaucratic' interference;
(iv) there has to be a local delivery mechanism because firms in less developed areas or regions do not tend to use distant 'national' facilities and institutions.

RESOURCES AVAILABLE LOCALLY

A large number and wide diversity of organizations and businesses have grown up over the years to promote, facilitate, and assist new enterprises being established and then their subsequent development. Some are in the private sector and some are in the public sector; some are commercial or, at least, charge fees while others are non-commercial or voluntary and community. Because a narrow view should not be taken of the type of agencies or organizations relevant to the formation and development of business at the smaller end of the size scale, only a brief overview — really a listing — of those currently or potentially available in Cork is possible here. A number of the state development agencies and organisations do not have regional or local offices — not to mind, of course, headquarters — located in Cork but do have a national remit which can be availed of in principle, if not easily in practice, by entrepreneurs in Cork on the same basis as those from any other part of the country. Since a number of the major agencies offer assistance and services that come under more than one of the three functional areas examined above, the listing is simply organized according to whether they are (primarily) at the Local/Regional, National, and European Community level. This outline for Cork is, more or less, representative of what is available elsewhere in Ireland.

Local/Regional Level

Local Authorities

Local Authorities are primarily concerned with the physical infrastructure of their areas. Both the County Borough and County Councils are actively — independently and jointly — involved in developing the physical and environmental infrastructure for business according to their development plans for land use. As well as this they collaborate with local promotional and representational organizations concerned with business and economic development. Since mid-1982 the County Council for example, has become more directly involved in promoting and facilitating small businesses within its existing resources by, for example, (i) the provision of reasonably priced serviced industrial sites, (ii) preparing for the provision of small (1,000 sq. ft.) low rental workshop units in a number of locations and (iii) the assignment of a Development Officer to assist business development. The County Borough Council is also exploring developments along similar lines.

In a number of towns throughout the county Urban District Councils are, to various degrees, becoming involved with helping the establishment of small scale enterprises which are mostly tourist and craft orientated. These are largely in response to the pressures from the increasing level of unemployment rather than as a systematic alteration in the direction of, and resources for, their development role. The legislative basis for local authorities appear to give them much wider statutory power, e.g. Section 77 of the Local Government (Planning and Development) Act 1963, to act as local economic development agencies, than any of them have exercised to date.

West Cork County Development Team

West Cork is one of the areas designated for special attention through County Development Teams. The operational agent of the team is a County Development Officer and it acts as the agent of the Industrial Development Authority. It administers a Discretionary Grants Scheme which, in certain circumstances, can provide small grants for activities not meeting the Industrial Development Authority's criterion for assistance.

Cork Harbour Commissioners

This is not concerned with promoting or facilitating small enterprises as such although it does provide incentives to firms who ship through the port in a substantial way by means of low rentals for office space and quay-side sites to facilitate assembly of goods.

South-West Regional Development Organization

This is a non-statutory coordinating office which is representative of local authorities and development agencies concerned with industry, tourism etc. in counties Cork and Kerry and fulfills a useful coordinating and advisory function for the entire South-West Region although the organization itself has very limited resources and relies primarily on the goodwill of its associated agencies and organizations.

Education Institutions

There are two substantial third-level educational institutions located in Cork city — Cork Regional Technical College (CRTC), which is under the aegis of the City Vocational Education Committee, and University College, Cork (UCC), which is a constituent college of the National University of Ireland. The CRTC is not as yet directly involved in the establishment or promotion of new small firms and is, primarily, an educational and research resource.

University College, Cork, has become more involved in recent years in promoting and facilitating enterprise creation and development through a number of channels. Its most recent and substantial commercial-orientated venture to date has been the founding of a wholly owned subsidiary company, Biotechnology (UCC) Ltd., to provide facilities for the transfer of new technology arising from biotechnology research and to develop new products and processes. It provides 'incubator' units for food product companies in its Food Science Complex. It is also the base for the national Microelectronics Research Centre which is concerned with semiconductor research in one of the best equipped laboratories of its type in Ireland and U.K. and has a number of links to industry through research contracts. The University has established an Industrial Liaison Committee and set up a Liaison Office with local business and agency representatives to develop new initiatives for its role in business and improving the local environment for business.

At the second level of educational institutions a few schools under different types of management, e.g. School of Commerce (CVEC) and Presentation Brothers, have promoted the business idea by informational courses and seminars to day pupils as well as to evening (adult) groups. The City and County Vocational Education Committees also offer a wide range of adult education courses, some of which are in activities amenable to commercial exploitation. In a few cases the focus has been on employment opportunities and addressed directly to the unemployed.

Banks; Finance/Investment Companies; Audit/Management Firms

Cork, primarily the city, has a substantial complement of private-sector banking, finance, and audit/management companies appropriate to an area of its size, population density, and industrial base. The organizations offer the usual range of services and, in a number of instances, have programmes tailored towards small business. But the small firm poses difficulties especially for the finance/investment firms and investment subsidiaries of the commercial banks. From the viewpoint of a large institution

- high administration costs;
- quality and frequency of management information inadequate due to lack of expertise on the part of small firms;
- limited resource base, which can be quickly depleted, and weak security position;
- lack of continuity through corporate structure in one-entrepreneur business — 'the entrepreneur living on adrenalin and driving his lenders to valium'.

A few of the larger Audit/Management companies offer service geared particularly towards small businesses in the areas of accounting, audit, management and project advice etc. But very often because they are branches of national or international institutions the orientation or skills of such companies may not be adequately geared towards the needs of a relatively small economy such as Cork. However, the financial institutions play a pivotal role in the economic development process and their capabilities and attitude can, in themselves, virtually determine the entrepreneurial tone of an area.

Labour and Business Associations

The representative associations for employers and employees are generally not directly involved in the process of enterprise creation and development and concentrate on their primary functions of representing the interests of their members. Indirectly, they are involved through their members assisting and encouraging, through formal or informal channels, in start-ups and development of small businesses and by their involvement in various forums and organizations, e.g. Cork Economic Development Council, Chamber of Commerce, which are concerned with the environment for business and economic development in Cork.

National Agencies and Organizations

There is a large number of state sponsored agencies charged with assisting enterprise creation and development, as part of general national industrial policy, or with providing more specialized services.

Industrial Development Agencies

There are three main industrial agencies operating in Cork or providing services available nationally.

INDUSTRIAL DEVELOPMENT AUTHORITY

The Industrial Development Authority (IDA) is the main national industrial development agency. It is in the process of regionalizing operations and has expanded its small industries section in Cork. This, if effective, over the long-term could be one of the most significant improvements in the local resource base for enterprise promotion. The main IDA programme relevant to our subject is the Small Industries Programme (SIP) which seeks to encourage the establishment and/or expansion of small enterprises meeting the IDA criterion for assistance, i.e. manufacturing (except activities deemed to be ones with domestic oversupply on domestic market) and some internationally traded services. Small firms are defined as having less than 50 employees or a fixed asset investment of less than IR£0·5m. The programme has a comprehensive package of incentives available covering capital grants, rent subsidy, training grants, sites and premises, working capital etc., product/process development grants, and feasibility study grants. In addition to the SIP there is an Enterprise Development Programme (EDP) to help suitably qualified people (e.g. engineers, accountants, scientists, business school graduates, experienced managers) establish enterprise for the first time, and includes assistances additional to SIP. The IDA also provides a number of other incentives, information, and promotion services (including an excellent 13 part 'kit' *Your Own Business*, providing an overview of basic informaton for business).

UDARAS NA GAELTACHTA; SHANNON FREE AIRPORT DEVELOPMENT COMPANY

Udaras na Gaeltachta has special responsibility for the Gaeltacht and its development approach and incentives programme is along the same lines as the IDA with whom it co-operates. Unlike the IDA, the Udaras is directly involved in the management of commercial companies.

The Shannon Free Airport Development Company (SFADCo) is concerned with industrial promotion in the Mid-West region only and its basic approach to development is similar to the IDA. SFADCo has also set up some specialised facilities and services which are available on a national basis and so, therefore, to the Cork area, e.g. a Training Division which, among its many services, conducts a six-month course on 'Entrepreneurship and High Technology' aimed at promoting, encouraging and training highly skilled potential entrepreneurs. Part of its function is to operate as a catalyst for entrepreneurial team formation by specialists in science, management etc. and so be the genesis of new technology-orientated enterprises.

Innovation Centre; Microelectronics Application Centre

The (national) Innovation Centre in Limerick provides a nationwide, fee-paying service based on project development, incubator/workshop, product identification, and innovation modules, and has been re-organizing its services in the light of experience and the changing environment in which it operates.

The National Microelectronics Application Centre, also located in Limerick, is concerned with promoting the use of microelectronics in industry either in product or processes. A range of fee-charged services are offered from product development (ideas, specification, design, prototyping etc.) to feasibility studies and ongoing servicing. The development work is carried out at the Centre, by the client company's own staff, or the specialist expertise of staff at the nearby National Institute for Higher Education can be consulted.

Institute for Industrial Research and Standards; National Board for Science and Technology

The Institute for Industrial Research and Standards is concerned with promoting the application of science and technology in a wide range of industry and covers a broad range of activities from packaging technology to energy conservation. It provides (i) technical advisory services designed to improve the efficiency of industry, (ii) services to identify and operationalize new technological opportunities under contract to clients, and (iii) R&D programmes in areas considered promising for Irish industry.

The National Board for Science and Technology is charged with the development of science and technology and, among a wide variety of activities, works with other state agencies, third level research and educational institutions and private sector companies to promote technological innovation in products and processes. It is involved in the formation of new, R & D orientated, enterprises in conjunction with Universities and private industry in, e.g., food biotechnology.

Coras Trachtala; other Marketing Agencies

Coras Trachtala/Irish Export Board (CTT) is the main state agency concerned with the promotion, assistance, and development of goods and services (except tourism and transport) exports. It provides a range of services, including a number of grants, and places a particular emphasis on assisting small firms. Two main categories of services are offered: Marketing (advice on markets, group promotion, and overseas offices) and Support (market research, trade information service, design and product development, publicity and publications, including a 13 part *Guidelines to Exporting*).

There are many other agencies and organizations concerned with product and market assistance and services to firms and include Bord Failte/Irish Tourist Board for the tourist industry, the Irish Goods Council serving all registered manufacturers, Crafts Council of Ireland providing advice and assistance to the Craft Industry, and Kilkenny Design Workshops developing new products and improving standards of design.

Anco/Industrial Training Authority; National Manpower Service; Youth Employment Agency

AnCO provides its services through three operating divisions: Training Advisory Services (concerned with employed persons and training within industry, especially small firms); External Training Division (largely concerned with unemployed persons) and the Training Centres Division (concerned with manpower skill training for unemployed or release employees). In the activity of enterprise creation AnCO provides 'Start Your Own Business' courses on a full-time basis for unemployed persons seeking to start up a business as well as a shortened evening version for those employed. This course takes people with a business idea through the basic stages, from market research to business plan, and is not confined to any particular lines of activity. A number of other courses and programmes are also offered for employees including managers, already or about to be made redundant, to assist them re-establish a career in employment or self-employment. Other courses are aimed at entrepreneurs in newly established enterprises (less than 3 years) who have to stay primarily involved in their business, as well as a whole range of courses in management training, product design and development, marketing etc. These courses are complemented by manpower and training services to firms to meet their labour needs. AnCO provides grants and allowances for these courses and acts as the training consultants to the Industrial Development Authority, etc.

The National Manpower Service is the employment agency of the Department of Labour and is primarily concerned with placement. However, the effect of the sustained recession has led to the development of new schemes aimed at self-employment, e.g. the Enterprise Allowance Scheme.

The Youth Employment agency operates a large number of programmes, through a variety of channels, which are relevant to enterprise creation. At present two programmes are directly concerned with enterprise establishment: the Youth Self-Employment Programme, operated through the Bank of Ireland, is a loan guarantee scheme to provide personally unsecured finance and enable borrowers to establish a credit record with the bank; the Community Youth Enterprise Programme is intended to encourage and assist local enterprise initiatives in both manufacturing and service areas by stimulating action by local community and youth organizations through the provision of grants and assistance, for example, to hire project leaders.

Industrial Credit Company

The Industrial Credit Company (ICC) provides a wide range of financial services to manufacturing, distributive and service enterprises on the usual basis for a development bank. It can, for example, provide capital through the purchase of share capital or as venture capital as well as financing working capital, equipment leasing etc. and it has a number of schemes for special needs, e.g. manufacturing exporters. In March 1984 the ICC introduced a new pilot scheme, the Cork Small Enterprise Scheme, aimed at promoting the establishment of new small businesses in the Cork area by providing a financial package which includes both equity and term loan finance. The ICC also have a Small Loan Scheme for Designated Areas.

Foir Teo, the state rescue agency, does not operate a scheme geared particularly towards the small firm which is in financial difficulties.

Irish Productivity Centre; Irish Management Institute etc.

A number of other organizations located in Dublin offer nationwide (occasionally on a regionalized basis) management training, consultancy and business services. For example, the Irish Productivity Centre, established by employer and labour unions, and the Irish Management Institute, a private (Government and E.E.C. supported) company, provide a comprehensive programme for management development and training and have a range of services geared towards small firms.

European Community

The European Community provides assistance to enterprises, industries, and areas through a large number of financial instruments in its major programmes, i.e. European Regional Development Fund, European Social Fund, and European Investment Bank, New Community Instruments.

Together with national governments, it operates an extensive range of programmes and has been developing new forms of assistance which are of particular relevance to the situation in Cork and local approaches to resolving the employment crisis. For example, a small, but useful, programme is outlined in Section 6 (Table 6.1) and, at the large scale, the recent changes in the operation of the regional policy are a significant improvement, which could be important for Cork, by allowing areas with integrated development plans direct access to the Commission for funding rather than having to go through the national authorities as hitherto.

IMPLICATIONS

The first part of this chapter reviewed, very briefly, the general requirements for enterprise creation and development at the smaller end of the size scale. This followed from the identification in Chapter 3 of such firms as having a key role in a community-based entrepreneurial strategy to generate employment in Ireland.

Most of the problems faced by small firms are not, of course, unique to small sized firms but they are exacerbated by the size factor and the pressure to grow under which many small firms must operate. The outline of the three broad requirements for enterprise creation and development highlighted, for example,

— the different issues arising for start-up and development of a business venture, e.g. importance of personal funds at the formation stage;
— the basic need to be forward looking and to plan, invest, and organize for change;
— the necessity to develop an entrepreneurial team with a suitable organization for strategic goal setting, decision-making, and effective implementation;
— the need to plan and make arrangements two to five years ahead of actual need;
— the importance of being integrated into a technology diffusion network to overcome obstacles to innovativeness arising from size and regional/peripheral location.

The development of a firm is usually not just a matter of becoming bigger and doing the same things in the same way as when the firm was smaller. It is a matter of qualitative change also and of making the necessary change in attitudes, organization, financial structure, products and technology etc. The development of a firm does not, obviously, have to take place autonomously but could also occur through takeover, sell-out, or merger approaches. The best strategic decision and arrangement among these options has also to be determined in each particular case.

Because of the recognition that small firms are important and may need a purpose-designed programme to meet their particular needs a whole array of organizations and agencies — mostly public sector — have been set up or arose to assist small firms. The second part of this chapter reviewed, again briefly, those available in Cork. Many of these have been available for some time. Others are of a more recent vintage and a few of those are a result of the employment crisis generally or the situation of Cork in particular. The resources as listed here don't meet all the needs which will have to be met. But, most importantly, neither does a basic listing of such resources by the agencies or organizations providing them convey the overall sense of how they are being deployed in Cork to create a local strategy.

There is no single direct means to generate employment on the scale urgently required. No one or two agencies or organizations can do it alone or even substantially alone. And it is not an issue of private *versus* state sectors or approaches. The answer lies in devising effective instruments, from appropriate combinations of the available resources, to create a framework which facilitates and encourages entrepreneurship and enterprise development. This will be seen from an explicit examination, in the following chapter, of the issues arising from the collation of the requirements and resources reviewed above. This exercise is approached on the basis of the strong impression which emerges from the review of resources that, so far as agencies and organizations go, especially those that are tax-payer funded, we have just about enough (if not already too much?) of everything; if all these do not work, or cannot be made to work, more of the same is very unlikely to bring an improvement. The perspective taken, therefore, is to focus on what is there already and to see what arrangements could be made, as a prelude to describing what arrangements are being made or explored, to effectively meet the needs identified.

5

Issues and Responses

The continually deepening economic crisis has been bringing about over the last few years a change in how the problem is perceived and, consequently, in the responses at both national and local levels. In the end the overall environment in which we operate is fundamental to having prosperity and, although only in very early stages as yet, there are some indications that national policy thinking is turning to face the entrepreneurial inadequacies which underlie the employment problem. Part of this is the realization that much more will have to be done at the local and community level than has been traditionally the case in Ireland.

As a reaction to the crisis the European Commission undertook a study and the Government, in January 1984, established a high level working group from a number of local authority and central government public agencies and organizations. In response to its Task Force report, the Government recognized the seriousness of the problems but pointed out that 'many of the problems of Cork are common to other areas which are heavily dependent on older industries; such problems are not unique to Cork but are more acute due to its dependence on large traditional companies, many of which have closed, cut back, or are now at risk'. In the light of constraints on the public finances, the Government action plan, in response to the Task Force Report, concentrated primarily on infrastructure. In the Dail the Minsiter for Industry, Trade, Commerce and Tourism, Mr. Bruton, pointed out that the number of jobs to be created would not depend on Government action alone and it was not a matter of creating jobs by government edict. The Government, he stated, were improving the infrastructure, and the number of jobs to be created depended, among other factors, on the response from Cork itself.

There can be no doubt that such a *local response* has been developing in Cork in cooperation with the national agencies and organizations and the European Community. This local response involves a wide range of elements and, in the following chapter, a *selection of those that bear a particular relationship to each other* are outlined to draw attention to the integrated nature of the framework to promote entrepreneurship which is currently emerging in Cork. To see the rationale for these developments, and the reinforcing relationship they have for each other, it is useful to stand back and look at the issues to be addressed and the general type of responses appropriate to them. In this chapter, with the previous reviews of requirements and resources for entrepreneurship and business formation and expansion at the small scale as the guide, appropriate instruments, and so possible responses, are identified to meet the issues arising. The segregation of this from what is currently occurring in Cork also permits gaps, which still need consideration, to be identified and so allows a more coherent overview, than would otherwise be possible at the present stage of development, to be given of the framework for entrepreneurship which is *emerging* in Cork. The latter is the subject matter of Chapter 6.

To devise a coherent strategy for entrepreneurship and enterprise creation and expansion requires recognizing, at the outset, that the needs of small enterprises are different throughout the phases of their formation and development. Therefore different expertise and assignment of responsibility by, or within, assisting agencies and organizations is required. There are, for example, a wide range of state agencies concerned with facilitating enterprise creation and development but the most important aids are confined to manufacturing, except if there is over-capacity, and some internationally traded services. There is less attention paid by private organizations due, largely, to the low direct return to such efforts. Thus, there is no systematic and sustained attention paid to the formation and development of firms in other lines of business activity. Furthermore, the need for leadership in attracting and harnessing resources among the local population requires an individual or group with a strong local orientation and commitment. This need could be met by establishing an Enterprise Creation Team to handle formation of enterprises and a Business Development Group, as part of a Business and Technology Centre, to manage growth after the small start-up. (These, and other instruments are outlined in Chapter 6).

The bottlenecks for small firms occur in all the major functional areas of a business, e.g. management quality, finance, innovation etc., and arise at creation and later development stages. There is, at its establishment, frequently a problem with the quality of the newly formed enterprise due to lack of skill, product inadequacy etc. Improving start-up businesses is not just a matter of providing more taxpayer funds as grants or loan guarantees. It is much more a matter of improving the quality of the personnel, product, financing structure etc., by advice and assistance, and doing so according to a business creation plan which is soundly based on production and costs, from which the financial or marketing projection exercises are really outcomes.

In response to the recession a number of new schemes, e.g. Enterprise Allowance Scheme, have been introduced and more are likely as the unemployment pressure continues. Many of these self-employment programmes are facilitating projects with little, if any, proper commercial evaluation and are facilitating largely one-person ventures in activities with little expansion potential or even long-term survival prospects. At best, many of these can only be viewed as facilitating learning 'to be in business' and as whetting of the appetite for entrepreneurship. This can, obviously, be quite important in itself but it is not obvious that the manner in which these are operationalised is the best and such programmes could easily result in widespread dissatisfaction over a longer time period.

There is a need to focus on getting entrepreneurs more soundly into business. The time and effort involved in what essentially are side issues to the core of business can be substantial despite — and even because of — all the assisting programmes and organizations. The 'threshold' costs of setting up a good quality small business could be substantially reduced by a small re-arrangement of some existing personnel and resources into an Enterprise Creation Team or teams to work with entrepreneurs seeking to found a business and establish a suitable organization.

There is nothing particularly sacred about smallness itself in a business. But again small firms, even in heavily assisted activities, find difficulties in developing due to inadequacies, e.g. in management which occur at points different from those many present aids and arrangements address. A more active approach to the development of existing small firms is necessary. It is also important that small firms see a coherent programme and approach for development to act as an encouragement to undertake what is a demanding task. A Business Development Group, as part of a Business and Technology Centre, could play an active role in this process and make a major contribution to the overall quality of new and expanding small enterprises.

There are many agencies and organizations involved in business promotion and assistance although many of them are limited in their lines of business activity which they can facilitate by services and grants. The plethora and complexity of this array gives rise to a fragmentation in entrepreneurial development of potential and actual entrepreneurs at the small scale level. This involves both gaps and overlaps. It also introduces the element of agency and organizational 'fiefdoms' that diffuses service and increases the costs of the overall effort. Coupled with this is the fact that the usual approach of most organizations is largely in the nature of performing 'staff' functions and have the attendant dilemma of authority without responsibility.

As much as is compatible with performing public service, the assistance delivery systems should approach 'line' involvement to bring effective service to the client, rather than organizational criteria and demands, to the forefront and to evalute effectiveness by real results — independent/commercial viability — for each firm over an appropriately long period. Despite all the assistance an entrepreneur is still very much on his or her own — especially in activities not meeting criterion for IDA assistance — at both the enterprise creation and, most especially neglected, later development stages. There is need to improve the institutional capacity to deliver services to potential and existing small businesses and to focus more coherently on people and organization than is the case at present where the effective emphasis although declining is on the physical aspects of an enterprise — buildings, equipment, product. This requires more direct, but appropriate, involvement with entrepreneurs in, and responsibility for, the creation of enterprises and their development such as would be provided by an Enterprise Creation Team at start-up stage and a Business Technology Centre at both start-up and later development stages.

Private and public sector agencies and organizations have different types of expertise and accountability criteria that could serve usefully to complement each other in the process of enterprise creation and development in Cork. Yet, however well the working relations are in practice, these complementary resources are not harnessed as effectively as they might and are often only done so informally. Also within the public sector there are organizations, e.g. educational institutions, which function according to quite different criteria than, for example, industrial development agencies. They may remain too distant from the entrepreneurial process. There is a need for intermediary arrangements which would bring the resources of those various organizations to bear in the most effective manner for enterprise creation and development without compromising the academic role which they must fulfill. There are a number of conceivable channels by which the necessary relationships could be arranged: Enterprise Creation Team, IDA Enterprise (Innovation) Centre, Business and Technology Centre, and facilitating in the coordination of Regional Management and Entrepreneurial Training Resources.

The recruitment pattern and skill distribution among longer term unemployed persons implies that a direct approach to promoting entrepreneurship and establishing good, soundly based enterprises is necessary and Community Area Enterprise Initiatives linked to the Enterprise Creation Team, Enterprise (Innovation) Centre, and the Business Technology Centre offers a direct network to bring entrepreneurship and the creation and development of modern technology based economic activities into areas not traditionally associated with such activities and currently neglected by the state and private organizations under arrangements existing hitherto.

The entrepreneur promotion instruments identified can be related to the three functional aspects under which the requirements for new, small enterprise formation and small enterprise development were outlined in Chapter 4. First, the central factor in entrepreneurial activity is people and the importance of the entrepreneurial team and appropriate organization has to be highlighted. And, as a result, there is a major need for more systematic attention to be paid to these aspects in the Cork area if the enterprise promotion process is to be most effective in getting businesses going on a small but significant scale. The emphasis on people has to be maintained with the development of business with potential for growth and the proven ability, willingness, and commitment for expansion. The need to approach these tasks in a coherent and planned way for each project must be emphasised because of the nature of the competitive environment in which firms seek survival.

Also the management, enterprise/business, and entrepreneurial training services in the area are inadequate and too diffuse to meet the needs for promoting a modern entrepreneurial economy. The entrepreneurial driven enterprise creation and employment expansion taking place in the U.S. today is due, to a significant degree, to the application of systematic management and entrepreneurial practices at the small firm level and in many traditional service activities. It is essential that new and small firms have access to the best skills they need, especially entrepreneurial and managerial, so that they can be innovative and competitive with larger domestic and foreign firms with greater internal resource bases and better access to external services with which to develop.

The basic thrust is to have the right people doing the right task within an organizational framework for expansion. It appears that much of this team development can be accomplished within a training context concerned with entrepreneurship and business formation which could be delivered through a combination of an Enterprise Creation Team, a Business Development Group within the Business and Technology Centre, and the better Coordination of Management and Entrepreneur Training Resources to focus on *enterprise* rather than *certification* .

A number of different schemes have been developed to encourage or provide long-term seed and risk finance for new, including small, enterprises, but, nevertheless, this remains a critical problem area for new small businesses and for their development. One approach has been to provide finance in return for an equity share but, from the viewpoint of a small firm with such good growth prospects, a 20% share, for example, is a lot of the business sold off at an early stage for what may turn out to be a relatively small capital contribution in many cases. A similar dilemma for the entrepreneur of a small enterprise can arise if the need for a short-term cash inflow pressures him or her, for example, into licensing a product developed by the entrepreneur. The longer term outcome may be to be shut out of potential markets or face competition with one's own product from a competing enterprise. Loan guarantee and cheap credit schemes, on the other hand, may result in commercially non-viable firms being propped up longer than they might otherwise survive. In such circumstances, a better return would be obtained by putting the resources into improving marketing, management capability etc. These financing schemes may help, but they have difficulties and, besides, they are not in themselves the answer. There is a need for personal funds to be committed to the venture, as well as alternative collective financing methods, and this is an area which has not received the attention it needs.

There is little point in recommending that banks, for instance, take greater risks; they are not in the business of unduly risking depositors and shareholders funds. This also very often reduces the actual effectiveness, as against hopes, of loan guarantee schemes. But risk is a matter of perception which can be reduced by better information on, and understanding of, a project and the people concerned. Rather than exhortation and bank-bashing, for these reasons, it would be more effective if suitable arrangements could be made to bring them into closer contact and involvement, from the point of risk finance, with the business formation and development process at the smaller scale. This could be brought about if the banking companies were to be involved in the Enterprise Creation Team and the Business and Technology Centre with its Business Development Group and Capital Funds.

The state, through a number of agencies, is also an important provider of seed capital and venture capital, especially in a tangible form as premises, advisory and training services, marketing and prototype development grants etc. and therefore it is desirable that any facilities provided, such as the IDA Enterprise Centre, be enhanced to the extent necessary for them to fulfill their purpose in the context of the needs of the Cork area.

Small and growing enterprises need convenient, appropriate sized, and flexible space arrangements and there are a number of ways of providing this, for example, 'in-house' in the Business and Technology Centre or decentralized in industrial units provided by the IDA and local authorities.

The requirement to be innovative — and not just in what is called 'high' technology products or processes — is crucial to the entrepreneurial dynamism of an economy but poses difficulties for small-scale enterprises and, more so, those in peripheral or regional areas. There is a need for an effective integration into the innovation-diffusion network and the active involvement of locally based research and educational institutions to link local entrepreneurship with newly developing technologies. The arrangements being highlighted here, enhancement of the IDA Enterprise Centre, the Business and Technology Centre with a Technology for Business Programme, and better regional Coordination of Management and Entrepreneur Training Resources, could meet these needs.

The purpose of outlining these issues, which arise from a comparison of the requirements and resources available for promoting and facilitating business creation and expansion in Cork, was to identify appropriate arrangements, *using presently available resources* which, taken together, could form a coherent response based on a local entrepreneurial strategy to the employment challenge. They are not, in themselves, sufficient and there are infrastructural and other needs which also have to be tackled. But they, or some things similar, appear to be necessary to insert an effective core into the specific task of promoting entrepreneurship in all lines of activity in Cork.

Over the last two or three years the increasing pressure of the crisis has been such that a clear vision of what is required has been emerging and this has led, in turn, to the available resources being adapted to meet the crisis. Although there is a long way to go yet — especially in changing public perceptions and attitudes and, particularly, in bringing the sense of esteem to entrepreneurship that is necessary to make Cork an entrepreneurial economy — developments are already underway, to varying degrees, on all but one (the Enterprise Creation Team) of the elements highlighted in this section. In the next chapter an overview of the integrated framework for entrepreneurship which can be discerned emerging in Cork is given. The purpose of this is, first, to provide some basic information on the various elements and, hence, the place of each element in a comprehensive strategy. Although the following account includes the Enterprise Creation Team it doesn't presume that this is the only, or even the best, way of filling the particular gap in the process for which it is intended. But some arrangement playing a similar role will probably be necessary and should, at least, be explored.[1]

[1] This aspect will be considered again in Chapter Seven.

6

The Emerging Framework for Entrepreneurship

The examination of the employment problem facing Cork and the reviews of the requirements and resources for an entrepreneurial-based local strategy to create employment identified five key elements. These were:

— Enterprise Creation Team(s)
— Enterprise (Incubation) Centre
— Business and Technology Centre
— Coordination of Entrepreneur and Management Training Resources
— Community Area Enterprise Initiatives

The discussion so far was conducted *as if none* of these elements were available, or developing, in Cork to show how the need for such instruments of entrepreneurial promotion and assistance arises. But, as already stated, Cork has already responded to the crisis and, specifically, the need to improve the entrepreneurial foundation of its economy. Although it is still early days yet, developments have already occurred or are occurring on all but the first element identified above:

— an enterprise centre is being developed by the Industrial Development Authority at its North Mall site in the City Centre;
— under the auspices of the Cork Chamber of Commerce a unique grouping of locally-based public sector agencies and institutions and private sector organizations, together with assistance from the Commission of the European Communities, is in the process of establishing a Business and Technology Centre;
— various groups concerned with management, training, and third-level education are examining the need for coordination and improvement of resources for entrepreneur and management training;

— in at least one city community area, without a tradition of entrepreneurship and lacking a business foundation to its economy, a community-based initiative to change all that in a fundamental way — rather than to seek temporary palliatives with high political visibility — is being worked out in cooperation with some public and private sector organizations.

These are not, of course, the only developments taking place which will improve the entrepreneurial environment in Cork. There are many others, ranging from small organizational matters to quite substantial infrastructural improvements, which will, when taken together, result in a significant transformation for enterprise and employment. Less easy to point to, but no less important for that, is the developing understanding and, as a result, the changing attitude occurring which will open up new opportunities and approaches that, at this stage, cannot be anticipated.

The elements highlighted here are selected not because they are the only or most important ones but because, by bringing these individual aspects together, it is possible to convey a sense of the *integrated nature of the framework for entrepreneurship which can be discerned emerging in Cork.* This chapter provides an overview of the type of developments which are occurring at present. The emphasis on *type of developments* is important because, since many of these are in early stages (and in one case is not occurring at all) the actual or final form cannot be detailed or presumed at this time.

The purpose of the discussion is therefore, first, to provide some general information on the purpose and operation of these aspects of the emerging entrepreneurial strategy and, second, to tentatively offer suggestions which might improve the overall effectiveness of the approach which is in the process of being created in Cork. Although it means starting with a 'gap' that needs to be filled, the presentation follows the order on the above list.

ENTERPRISE CREATION TEAM

Getting going in business on a sound base, and with good potential for growth, is not an easy matter for an entrepreneur today for a number of reasons including, it must be emphasised, some which are 'self-inflicted'. There is a need at present, and at least for some years in the future, for a deliberate and direct intervention by public *and* private sector organizations, with complementary skills, in the very earliest stages of entrepreneurship in Cork as part of the strategy to change attitudes and improve business creation. One way to do this would be to establish an Enterprise Creation Team or Teams to be actively involved in the process of creating a business. The purpose of such a group is not to replace existing agencies and services but to provide an arrangement whereby they can come together to actively seek out growth opportunities which may currently be lost and assist in their initial development. It could do this by:

- working actively with potential entrepreneurs who already have a business idea or need to identify a business idea;
- identifying business ideas desirable for the Cork economy and seeking out suitable entrepreneurs to implement them; and it should be particularly concerned with working directly with groups of unemployed persons on a programme of entrepreneurial and business-manpower skill development which is intended to culminate in the foundation of a business;
- searching among existing single proprietorship and small scale enterprises for those with the potential, and willingness, for further development; and
- being concerned with *all lines of business activity*, as it would be concerned with the overall business mix in Cork, and therefore not confined to manufacturing and services meeting criteria for assistance laid down in the national industrial policy guidelines for the IDA etc.

Primarily it would directly work with an entrepreneur on ideas with potential for high growth and employment but which require extensive and detailed preparation. It provides a means whereby (i) state agencies and authorities charged with development could be more effective at an earlier stage than at present and (ii) the distance between private and public sector organizations can be bridged, with their different skills and motivations harnessed for a coordinated effort, to improve the quality and, hopefully, the number of enterprise start-ups in Cork.

A key aspect of the Enterprise Creation Team's job would be to prepare *with* the entrepreneur a thorough business formation plan for the establishment and early development of an enterprise. Nowadays, such a plan has to be comprehensive and cover all aspects of the new firm — product, process, personnel and organization, premises, equipment, supplies, production, marketing and financing structure and sources for the start-up — in order to obtain financing and other necessary resources from public and private sector agencies and institutions. As well as setting specific goals such a plan sets out in detail the means and schedule by which they are to be achieved, e.g. for the development of a product: what development is necessary? how, where, and by whom can it be carried out? What development of personnel in the operative, administrative and managerial categories is required by recruitment of persons and/or the design of a training programme using appropriate public and private agencies and organizations? Such assistance is required so that the plans are properly based on the production side of the business and not just on the — often very optimistically formulated — marketing side which is too often the case.

Setting up such a team does not imply a presumption that every new firm is going to grow into a large scale enterprise. Its purpose is to ensure new firms are created on the basis of an appropriate plan to facilitate its formation and early development by addressing whatever needs and obstacles can be anticipated at the outset. Obviously not all new firms will or can become large scale enterprises or internationally competitive with an accompanying significant level of employment. But it is crucial that those with the potential (perhaps 1 in 100 possibilities?) should be facilitated as early as possible, and not lost in the early formative period due to obstacles or events which could be removed or overcome with appropriate and timely action. But overall *the role of such a team is to improve the quality of entrepreneurship* in its early stages in Cork.

In the context of the overall framework emerging in Cork, firms developed by the Enterprise Creation Team could be at any of a number of stages, for example:

— they may need to develop product or process up to a commercial state and so may be referred, for example, to the Enterprise (Incubation) Centre being developed by the Industrial Development Authority;
— they may be established at what is expected to be at optimum scale and organization and can be set up in appropriate premises etc., which could be on an Industrial Development Authority industrial estate or in a Local Authority business unit which are not confined to designated manufacturing or service activities
— they may have potential for further development and could be referred to the Business and Technology Centre which is in the process of being established for that purpose.

It is obviously crucial that entrepreneurs be deeply committed to their projects and involved in all stages of their preparations. The Enterprise Creation Team would work *with* the entrepreneurs. As it is at present the establishment of a business venture on any significant scale is a daunting venture if for no other reason, but there are many others, than the wide diversity of state agencies and government regulations to be handled. Successful negotiation of these stages may only indicate ability to handle administrative organizations and does not necessarily prove entrepreneurial ability to succeed in competitive markets. Nor are the skills acquired in crossing bureaucratic hurdles those needed to create *entrepreneurial* enterprises. The potential entrepreneur has to go through various preparatory stages, and probably will involve personal development as much as anything else, which may be unavoidable or desirable. The benefits from establishing one or more Enterprise Creation Teams would be that:

— costs, difficulties, and delays of getting into business can be eliminated or reduced by a team devoted to this task and with the necessary skills and, thereby, the entrepreneur is allowed to focus on the crucial matters for his or her contribution to the business;
— over time a team will build up expertise, local knowledge, and experience which otherwise would be diffused throughout many public and private sector organizations;
— the entrepreneurs firms or products with potential for substantial growth may be identified and facilitated earlier than might otherwise be the case without an active involved approach;
— it is not confined to manufacturing and services designated for assistance by national industrial policy and so actively promotes and assists the creation of enterprises in non-designated activities as well as complementing the efforts in designated lines of business.

In the light of the issues raised in Chapter 5 an Enterprise Creation Team to meet the needs identified, could be established on the following basis without adding to tax-payers costs:

— A team could be organized by a Local Authority and formed in conjunction with public and private sector organizations relevant to the creation of business enterprises;
— ideally, perhaps, there could be at least two separate teams based on the Borough Council and the County Council. However, given the resource constraints which these — as well as other organizations — will face in the foreseeable future, the experimental nature of such an arrangement, and because it is essential that a team be staffed with personnel of the highest calibre, one such team could be formed jointly by the two Local Authorities and, at the outset, it could possibly focus on the Greater Urban Area which has the highest concentration of population and unemployment in Cork;
— The team could consist of persons from relevant public sector organizations such as the Borough and County Councils, Industrial Development Authority and AnCO/Industrial Training Authority, and two persons from the relevant private sector organizations, i.e. commercial banks involved in financing small business and major auditing/management consultancy companies involved with new and small scale enterprises. It would be desirable that one of the persons from the latter organizations have expertise in the areas of financing the start-up stages, as well as general finance, of small, growing enterprises;
— All personnel could be on secondment from their own organizations for periods of, say, not less than two years, and, therefore, be funded by these organizations. With the exception of the Borough Council, the state agencies already have personnel assigned similar

activities and it is quite possible that, at least, one of the larger banks and audit/management companies might favourably consider such a contribution to improving the overall entrepreneurial environment in Cork;

The public sector agencies listed above are already statutorily assigned developmental duties which can encompass their contribution to such a team. The private sector organizations however are not responsible for promoting such general activities and are charged with earning income for their shareholders. Their involvement in an Enterprise Creation Team

TABLE 6.1

Community Supported 'Better Business Service' in Strathclyde

'Better Business Services' is provided by a New Strathclyde Consultants Consortium which is a grouping of financial institutions, business advisors, employers' representatives and local business development organizations willing to help towards the common objective of improving business performance.

It is a collection of nine services to improve three key business functions: Management and Administration, Financial Management, and Sales Marketing. At Strathclyde this comprises:

1. *Management and Administration Services*
   General Check-up
   Management Planning and Organization Service
   Business Administration for Small Firms
   Start-Ups Service
2. *Financial Management*
   Financial Investigation and Restructuring Service
   Expanded Business Plan Service
   Profit Improvement Studies
   Management and Financial Control Systems
3. *Sales and Marketing*
   Sales and Marketing Plan
   Translation Service for Exporters

The key management functions, with the exception of production, are covered. The 'Better Business Service' operates by subsidising the *direct use of the services* by smaller companies. The 'Better Business Service' is substantially funded by the European Community under the *non-quota* section of the European Regional Development Fund. The subsidy is, under European Community criteria for the non-quota section of the European Regional Development Fund, 55%. Another 20% must come from the company and the balance of 25% from the small firm or other source. The latter could be made up by agencies and organizations in the public and private sector.

could yield significant benefits — directly attract clients, indirectly obtain business as a result of a stronger local economy, and, especially in the case of a bank, improve their members' expertise in the area of new business formation and small business development in Cork. (This involvement in a team would provide banks with an effective and visible means of reducing their exposure to frequent charges that they lack knowledge, understanding and interest in the local economy, and exhortations to do more, where the 'more' is usually unspecified and vague). However important these benefits may be they will hardly earn a significant short-term financial return on their contribution to the team. Because the outlay on this activity, which they would not normally undertake, is substantial consideration would have to be given to means by which they can at least be partly compensated.

The preparation of a business formation plan, and other start-up work, will involve a number of subsidiary studies and consultations which are eligible for grant aid from various agencies. Where appropriate these could be assigned to the bank and audit/management firm contributing to the Enterprise Creation Team and thereby serve as partial recoupment of their outlay. At present the Industry Committee of the Chamber of Commerce has organized an informal, and free, advisory service provided by members of the Chamber, for people interested in setting up their own business which is complementary to those available from the established development agencies. Perhaps the possibility of setting up a 'Better Business Service', for instance, along the lines of the one presently operating in Strathclyde, Scotland with significant European Community funding, summarized in Table 6.1, could be examined. In itself the availability of such a service in the Cork area is highly desirable and would be an important complement to the Enterprise Creation Team. But it could also provide a source of revenue to the private sector organizations participating in the Enterprise Creation Team.

The Enterprise Creation Team is probably only one of a number of possible ways which could meet the particular needs of *improving the entrepreneurial potential* of the area, i.e. prior to the start-up. Therefore, the *experimental nature of this particular suggestion should be emphasized.* It is an experiment to address, in an active way, the simultaneous processes of helping to create opportunities locally and encouraging entrepreneurship. It could be established, initially, on a pilot basis for five years and its effectiveness subject to careful evaluation at the end of that time to determine whether it should be continued. A period less than five years would probably be insufficient because a team such as this which is concerned with a very complex process — that of business creation — will need a period of learning to determine its most effective mode of operation. To be effective it would have to be seen to operate as an active 'on the road' unit rather than be office or desk bound 'waiting for clients'. It should be evaluated by criteria reflecting its purpose, i.e. the formation of commercially viable enterprises, and not by the number of 'clients' handled as is too often the case with public sector agencies and state supported organizations. The evaluation would have to take into account the type, quality, and scale of enterprises and not just the number. The number indeed could *appear* to be quite small although, in effect, the improvement of entrepreneurship in the local economy might be very significant. What would be deemed an acceptable annual rate of new small firms could appear quite low if the emphasis is placed on 'good' new firms. It is something which would have to be discovered in practice. The term 'good' refers to judgements concerning product, organization, personnel, and financial structure and, most importantly, potential for survival and growth. The team would, of course, be involved in preparing the start-up package for many other new ventures but it is the potential for commercially sustained growth which is the most significant criterion. Any evaluation would be concerned with how near the actual results correspond to the projected outcomes and anticipated growth potential and could only be carried out after a time period sufficient for the potential for survival and expansion projected at the start-up stage to be realized. It could not, therefore, be done on an annual 'clients' basis.

ENTERPRISE (INCUBATION) CENTRE

The provision of premises and grant support for product development and related matters are the most important means by which state development agencies can provide *risk capital* to emerging enterprises. The Enterprise Centre being developed by the Industrial Development Authority, at the North Mall in the City Centre, will be significant in the entrepreneurial environment locally because it will provide incubator facilities for new small scale enterprises in the initial stages of product development. The resources planned for the Enterprise Centre are:

- premises will consist of 30,000 sq. ft. with units in the range of 250 sq. ft. to 500 sq. ft. which would be suitable for 1-6 persons. The rental rate will be at the Industrial Development Authority's rate for Cork (IR£2.40 per sq. ft.) and this will be eligible for the IDA rental subsidy;
- the centre will operate as an incubator facility, i.e. according to an 'up and out' philosophy, with the maximum tenancy set at about 2¾ years. Tenancies for as little as 1 month can be obtained and will be based on an 'easy out' arrangement;
- only activities which meet the criteria for assistance of the Industrial Development Authority will be eligible for the Enterprise Centre

and the entrepreneur will be eligible for the usual range of assistance;

— some, very basic, business services will be available on a shared ('pay-as-used') basis. The Enterprise Centre will have a general manager, on a full-time assignment from the Industrial Development Authority, who will be available to assist entrepreneurs.

An indication of the scale of the planned facility in Cork can be gauged from the summary information of the Pearse Street, Dublin Enterprise Centre which, it should be noted, is much more than an incubator enterprise centre. A summary outline of the Pearse Street Centre is given in Table 6.2.

While, obviously, the Enterprise Centre is in itself a welcome addition to the Industrial Development Authority's instruments for manufacturing promotion in Cork there is, nevertheless, a need to develop it further or, alternatively, to find some complementary way to provide for the requirements of small enterprise creation and development, especially the need to improve access to the commercialization of modern technological innovations as well as other business development resources. The intended resources do not appear to be adequate for the development of high quality new products and business ventures. In particular, the planned services would need to be expanded to include a more active involvement in the development of the new business. Also more assistance and facilities are required for addressing technological aspects of products or processes if it were to serve as an effective *innovation* facility which is needed for the Cork economy. An urgent need is to improve access to technological innovation networks at home and abroad and to ensure rapid commercial exploitation of perceived opportunities.

The effectiveness of the Enterprise Centre could be enhanced as an innovation facility in a number of ways. For example, an Enterprise Creation Team could actively assist the entrepreneurs in the creation of their business and facilitating the initial start-up phase of a new enterprise. Indeed, having a group such as an Enterprise Creation Team is probably a prerequisite to ensure the optimum use of the centre as an incubation facility. Other agencies and organizations with expertise in the area of product and process technology could also be brought into active involvement with the enterprises developing within the Centre. For example, the national agencies with assigned responsibility in the area of technology for business, i.e National Board for Science and Technology and Institute for Industrial Research and Standards, and the educational institutions, e.g. University College, Cork — with its National Microelectronics Research Centre and food research facilities — and the Regional Technical College, Cork could be involved actively in the programmes of the centre. The establishment of close ties with the proposed Business and Technology Centre and its

TABLE 6.2

Industrial Development Authority Enterprise Centre, Pearse St., Dublin 2

PURPOSE: To provide business services and production space.

FACILITIES:

(i) *Premises*

Industrial estate on 5·2 acre site providing, approximately, 17,250 square metres of individual floor space — 14,850 square metres in 35 manufacturing units ranging from 100 to 1,950 square metres and 2,400 square metres in 'The Tower' (a renovated 19th century sugar refinery) in units of various configurations ranging from 16 square metres to 88 square metres.

(ii) *Business Services*

Basic administrative and secretarial services are provided on a pay for use basis by a firm employing 5 persons. Services include typing, word-processing, photocopying and telex.

A full-time IDA manager, who manages the Centre, is available to provide project advice and guidance and to arrange professional assistance in marketing, design etc.

A small accountancy firm, for which specific advertisement was made, is resident in the Tower.

(iii) *Incubator Units*

Eight incubator units were opened in July 1983 to provide facilities for up to two years in order to cater for product development, and facilitate licence acquisition, market surveying, arrangement of joint ventures, and production start-up. Size ranges from office with desk and telephone to 88 square metres manufacturing units. Short-term leases available.

(iv) *AnCO/The Industrial Training Authority Courses*

AnCO provides its 'Start Your Own Business' course on a day and evening basis and emphasises business management and development with particular emphasis on first-type businesses.

ELIGIBILITY: Meet IDA sectoral criteria and aid requirements.

OPERATION:

(i) The Enterprise Centre is part of the IDA programme for industrial renewal and job creation in the inner city area of Dublin. Local community involvement is introduced via cooperatives operating the Administrative/Secretarial Services and Canteen facilities.

(ii) Space is rented at the IDA Dublin rental rate (£29·60 per square metre p.a.). The running costs of the Tower Centre IDA facilities (manager, caretaker etc.) is paid for by a charge of £5·90 per square metre p.a. on Tower units and £4·80 per square metre p.a. on outer units.

(iii) The Administrative/Secretarial firm charges on a user basis and about 90% of its business comes from other firms in the Centre. It is a viable business which reinvests profits in expanding equipment and facilities. At present it is managed by an IDA nominee.

(iv) As of April 1984, approximately 400 persons were gainfully employed in the Centre — 23 businesses located in the outer units and 30 (mostly single proprietorship firms) located in the Tower.

(v) The incubator unit, operating since July 1983, but only filling up over next few months, had produced one enterprise up to mid-1984.

(vi) The Tower houses the joint advisory and administrative services, an accounting firm, exhibition, reception and meeting areas, shop, canteen, incubator units, AnCO, 1 large craft workshop (318 square metres) and 24 craft workshops (16-88 square metres). The craft projects occupy over half the space.

Technology for Business Programme, as well as close liaison with its Business Development Group would provide Cork with a substantial — but no more than necessary — method for technology acquisition. This would also be desirable for the smooth transition and further development of enterprises to be referred to the Business and Technology Centre or to be provided with its services.

The opening of the Enterprise Centre, as currently proposed by the Industrial Development Authority, was delayed pending planning appeals and by a 'temporary' cancellation by the Government and this has been costly when the process of getting a new good business going is borne in mind. Every single good firm with potential for growth matters. Even when open it will be about two further years, at least, before the first new firms 'graduate' from the Centre. Thus, as of now, there is a gestation period of about three years before it can begin to have a direct input into the economic revitalization of the Cork economy. This Centre can make a significant contribution to that task and, even more so, if it can be enhanced and become an integrated part of the emerging entrepreneurial framework in Cork. Nevertheless, even if this is done, its operation will still be constrained by the criteria laid down in the national industrial policy within which the IDA has to operate.

BUSINESS TECHNOLOGY CENTRE

The most important gap, identified in Chapter 5, in the existing range of programmes and instruments for business promotion in Cork is the area of *development of an enterprise in any line of business activity.* The various elements involved — personnel, organization and management; product ideas, development, and marketing; and finance — were all addressed in on form or another, primarily for manufacturing. However, the overall result at present is still a lack of focus, and hence thrust, in the promotion of a modern, entrepreneurially orientated economic base in Cork.

If an Enterprise Creation Team were to be organized and the Enterprise Centre being developed by the Industrial Development Authority were substantially enhanced some of the gaps would be closed. But these relate to the early stages of initiating business ventures and creating and establishing enterprises which are at the smaller end of the scale. *They do not address the later stages which are crucial to the survival and expansion of small enterprises.* Most significantly, from the point of view of employment in the longer term, they are not available for helping to actively expand firms which could become major employers in the area. An approach which could overcome this is the Business and Technology Centre.

A Business and Technology Centre (BTC) is made up of four elements:

— Business Development Group
— Premises and Business Administration Services
— Technology for Business Programme
— Capital Funds

As will be apparent these are available in one form or another at present but are not brought together in a coherent and active manner to meet the full development needs of all small firms in the Cork area. Since this is a new approach which is developing both in Ireland as well as in other countries, an outline of the most important general features of a BTC is given below under these headings. As the preparatory work for the first Cork BTC has only begun there is obviously no presumption intended about the specific form which will be decided for it. At the beginning of 1985 preparatory work has begun with primary funding from the European Commission. It is being carried out by a group composed of both public and private sector organizations under the auspices of the Chamber of Commerce. The group includes, from the public sector, County and County Borough local authorities, Industrial Development Authority, National Board for Science and Technology, and University College, Cork; from the private sector the Chamber of Commerce and the Cork Council of Trade Unions are presently involved. A project manager has been appointed to work with the sponsoring group to carry out the preparatory work.

Business Development Group

A core feature of the Business Development Group is that there is a *team* of people with the expertise to assist, and the responsibility for working with, small enterprises to bring them beyond their initial stages. This is not a question of 'hand-holding'. Rather it is an involvement and commitment to bringing firms up to their full potential. It provides this service for all firms in the Business and Technology Centre. But it also seeks and develops those rare opportunities — perhaps the 1 in 100 — that can become major successes and so its operation is founded on the hope that a few large, highly profitable, and job creating, ventures will emerge and can be developed from its 'portfolio' of firms.

The composition of a Business Development Group is arranged so as to bring together a team with complementary skills to service the overall needs which growing firms have. This would, therefore, include persons with the following expertise:

— Chief Executive (group leader and manager of BTC company)
— Management/Administration — Organization
— Technology (especially identification and legal aspects e.g. patents, transfer, and licensing)
— Product (design, development, and marketing)
— Finance (especially seed capital and venture capital)

It is increasingly accepted, and even required, that the expansion of each firm should be undertaken on the basis of a comprehensive plan for the development of the enterprise. A Business Development Plan has to cover all aspects (such as product design, marketing, and production; identification and access to technologies and their implementation; personnel and organizational development; premises and equipment; and financial structure and sources of funds) during the various stages of expansion. This plan could be prepared by the Business Development Group *and* the entrepreneur(s) in a firm. It serves two purposes. First, the process involved in preparing the plan is a vital stage in the entrepreneurial development of the personnel for a business; the stages must occur anyway for a firm to expand; planning it coherently and systematically provides a stronger information and decision foundation for expansion. Second, it provides this stronger foundation by (i) explicitly identifying goals, requirements, means and potential obstacles, and (ii) setting a stages programme for development that identifies the tasks to be accomplished at each stage, procedures for monitoring, and criteria for evaluating performance. Ongoing monitoring and diagnosis, as well as a continuous planning review, are also features of the collaborative approach of the Business Development Group with the enterprise directors and managers. These services could be offered to firms which are not 'tenants' of the Business and Technology Centre and so the BTC fills a major need in the entrepreneurial process in Cork.

Premises and Services

The Business and Technology Centre offers suitable and flexible space on easy leasing terms to facilitate the needs of small firms as they expand or contract. The Centre does not operate according to an up and out philosophy and firms may find it suitable as a permanent home. However, as the Business and Technology Centre itself operates on a commercial basis, it must manage its 'portfolio' of firms so that there is a sufficient proportion of firms with growth potential. An advantage of the flexible space policy of the BTC is that firms can expand or contract, according to their needs and resources, without having to incur the costs of changing location.

As well as commercial tenants, it is likely that various state agencies and private organizations concerned with industrial development and business would want to locate in the same premises if space were available. This is because a Business and Technology Centre comes to be perceived as a business opportunity and support centre and can play a useful role in integrating business and entrepreneurship into the community. Thus, for example, agencies such as AnCO/Industrial Training Authority, Industrial Development Authority, Coras Trachtala/Irish Export Board etc., may find it a convenient base for some operations. It could also be the base for an Enterprise Creation Team which would facilitate cooperation between this group, with responsibility for enterprise promotion and creation, and the Business Development Group, which is responsible for the development of enterprises after their initial stages.

Access to high quality business services is not a luxury for modern businesses, especially those concerned with foreign trade, but is something small firms cannot afford themselves or find costly and inconvenient to purchase from outside companies. The Business and Technology Centre makes available on a common basis the wide range of administrative, secretarial, graphic, communication, translation etc. services which are now a necessary part of conducting a business. This would be particularly important where small Irish firms have to try to break into foreign markets. All business administration services are paid for by each firm according to the use made of them. Again these can be available to firms outside the Business and Technology Centre.

Technology for Business Programme

Searching and arranging for new technologies and then implementing them successfully is beyond the resources and expertise of most small firms. Also the marketing and selling of technologies developed by the small firm itself is probably beyond the resources and, more often than not, the interests (although profitable) of the small firm entrepreneur. The Business and Technology Centre provides a mechanism for the inflow and outflow of technology by having a person skilled in the area of searching and arranging technologies for businesses, and by supporting this person with the skills and resources necessary to obtain or market technology locally, nationally, and internationally. The role of this person is not just to identify a suitable technology but also to make the best legal transfer arrangements to meet a firm's need whether that involves licensing, joint venture etc. The service provided to firms also includes the access to and holding of information materials, such as marketing data, relating to market and product opportunities and other current information sources which help to inform and identify opportunities and obstacles. This service would also function as an ideas and support centre for new entrepreneurs.

The local development of applied technologies is fundamental to the long term industrial competitiveness of Cork. To this end a Business and Technology Centre also provides appropriate methods for the University and the Regional Technical College and the national organizations, (national) Innovation Centre, Institute of Industrial Research and Standards, and National Board for Science and Technology (some of whom have regionalized facilities) to be effectively involved in improving the prosperity of the local economy. They not only benefit indirectly from the more prosperous environment but also benefit directly from the utilization of facilities — which otherwise they might not be able to fund — and the involvement of staff in business application of their professional skills and knowledge.

Capital Funds

Related to the creation and development of small enterprises, for which a key requirement is the transfer of technology, is the resources and means for funding these activities at the various stages in the life-cycle of a firm. Raising the various forms of risk capital poses particular difficulties for setting up new and, especially, small firms. And these types of funding are essential even where the new application of known technologies and product development are involved. As pointed out in connection with the Enterprise Centre discussed already, the state agencies can provide substantial amounts of seed and venture capital in the form of 'non-perishables' e.g. training for persons. But there are limited sources for such risk finance, and the extent to which tax-payers funds can be ventured for commercial activities has to be very circumscribed.

Furthermore, the promoted venture capital funds do not adequately meet the needs of an entrepreneur who has an idea and nothing else. At the very least a proven track record in business generally, and even the specific activity or technology in question, is invariably sought. That may not be too serious if the pool of potential entrepreneurs with experience is quite large. It is certainly a problem if it is a question of promoting and facilitating people in their first venture as is very likely to be the case in Cork. But also, the finance is usually only for ventures in a few particular lines of activity.

The final component which is essential to the overall Business and Technology Centre approach is, therefore, the arranging and, if necessary, the provision, of different types of finance. Because the Business Development Group is actively involved with the entrepreneur it is less concerned with established track records and credit ratings than might other funders. As is usually the case with such finance, it is provided on an equity share basis. It is important that the Business and Technology Centre have equity in firms for both internal incentive reasons — it is a commercial operation — and for the long term growth of its capital funds. The Centre will build up a portfolio of investments in firms with growth potential. As the firms outgrow the Centre and its services the shares may be liquidated to replenish and expand the capital funds for further investment in new growth orientated firms, i.e. the BTC can realize its investments and re-invest the proceeds in new growth projects.

The role of the finance manager would also extend to advising on and arranging other types of short term and long term equity and loans, as well as drawing together the full financial implications of the product, production, and technology aspects of the Business Development Plan.

Concept of Business and Technology Centre

The Business and Technology Centre is itself a business and constituted as a company. It is primarily in the business of business development, i.e. of servicing small firms that want to grow and develop to the full potential of the people and the enterprise. As a commercial venture it would have to at least break even on its operational costs. (The capital outlay may in some cases be treated, partly or fully, as infrastructural investment to facilitate economic development of the area.)

A number of Centres with, to varying degrees, the services outlined above have been operated for some years in the United States by the Control Data Corporation of Minneapolis, Minnesota and use the registered-name 'Control Data Business and Technology Centre'. They have also been involved in the development of, or preparation for, similar type centres at Stevenage in the U.K. and Liege in Belgium. Their expectation is that such centres, properly established, should break even on current operating costs in about 5 years. However, there is included in the scheme here, as possibly the most important single element, the Business Development Group which is not included in Control Data Centres. But this appears to be necessary in Cork to close a major gap in the arrangement of resources to promote the entrepreneurial development and the expansion of firms with growth potential. Variations along BTC lines have also been developed in, for example, the U.K. by British Steel Corporation (Industry) Ltd. and in the Netherlands by the Phillips Job Creation project and there are a number of state and private sector developments along such lines beginning in Ireland, for example, the I.D.A. Enterprise Centre at Pearse St., Dublin and Job Creation Ltd at the Kildare Enterprise Centre in Kildare.

The sources of revenue for the Centre come from providing the services of the four elements outlined: (i) rental for premises and charges for business administration services; (ii) fees for the services of the Business Development Group (which firms could partly meet by equity sharing and by grants from state combined with Community sources; (iii) fees from the Technology for Business Programme; and (iv) dividends and capital gains on investment portfolio. The provision of these services need not be confined to firms in residence in the Business and Technology Centre and so the revenue earning base is larger than just from in-house clients.

A Business and Technology Centre would be a vital complement to the present range of promotional services by filling a major gap in the resources available for small business creation and development in Cork. But it is also largely a new development for Ireland and so there will, of course, be many difficulties to be resolved on the way to its establishment and smooth operation. Because it is itself a business company its establishment will involve arranging a consortium among relevant public sector and private sector agencies and organizations with a view to financing and operating such a centre. In particular it is a very effective way for local banking and management/audit institutions to be actively involved in the process of business creation and development at the small end of the size scale without incurring undue costs and unacceptable risks. As well as these private and public sector organizations, whose 'investment' in the Centre may be due through the provision of services or facilities, there are other sources of funding. For example a Business and Technology Centre — premises and activities — may be eligible for European Community and national government co-financing. Also, for example, the Control Data Corporation and British Steel (Industry) Ltd. have been involved in complete or substantial funding of many activities, along BTC lines, to replace lost jobs. Both of these initially became interested in developing business and technology centres because they sought to reduce the impact of plant closures on their communities and focussed attention specifically on utilizing large vacant premises. Similarly, it may be possible to get companies shutting down major plants in Cork to consider equity investment in the Centre to alleviate the impact of closing down on the area and to avoid the depressing effect of empty industrial premises. Similarly, in other parts of Ireland the BTC approach could be followed when faced with the closure of large industrial plants.

Much expertise has been built up in recent years by such companies as Control Data Corporation of Minneapolis, British Steel Corporation (Industries) Ltd., and Phillips Job Creation project in The Hague in the development of such centres, and the tackling of many 'inner city' type problems which appear to be particularly relevant to many of the difficulties facing Cork. Their experiences can be utilized to facilitate developing the Cork BTC. Also these companies are obviously familiar with high technology and, increasingly, with its transfer outside the innovating company and between firms. The skills and knowledge they have learnt will vary because of the different problems and contexts with which they were concerned and this can also help with the design of a BTC. For example, the U.S. company may have insights, derived from experience in the highly entrepreneurial U.S. economy, which may be useful in developing an entrepreneurial economy in Cork. Thus tapping the expertise of these companies in the preparatory work could result in a substantial transfer of the 'technology' of such centres to Cork. Furthermore, many domestic state and private organizations already have expertise in aspects of the activities of a BTC which will further help the design of a suitable facility for Cork.

The matter of actual location and premises is also important. There are two approaches: a new, purpose built construction or adaptation of an existing vacant industrial building, and the costs and benefits of both have to be assessed. Without presuming the outcome of that examination, which will have to look into factors which are not relevant here, the role of a BTC approach in revitalizing old industrial plant is worth examining because developments such as these have often begun as a response to the shutdown of large enterprises:

— a Business and Technology Centre fills up slowly and an existing building can be adapted as the occupancy rate increases, so the heavy outlay for constructing a whole new building can be avoided;
— it is already there and is vacant, so the owners may be willing to sell at a reasonable price because of commitment to the Cork area or expectation that it will be difficult to sell otherwise;
— some of these currently vacant are in good central locations in the Greater Cork Urban Area. The location of a Business and Technology Centre close to population and commercial activity is beneficial both to the Centre and the industrial revitalization of the economic base of the urban area;
— some of these premises would provide space for a Business and Technology Centre of, say, 150,000 sq. ft. net leasable, adequate space for Centre facilities and business services, space for other organizations and agencies attracted to the developments in the Centre, and, if one can be found, one or more larger scale operations or activities with sub-supply needs;
— the negative effect of empty and decaying buildings, associated with older and failed industries, on confidence and entrepreneurship and appearance of an area is significant and it is desirable, if at all cost effective, to breath new life into these rather than let the decay continue to drag more down.

The premises are only the physical manifestation of a Business and

Technology Centre which is, ultimately, a *process* of entrepreneurial activity. But the premises and its location can contribute enormously to its success and thereby its effectiveness as an instrument of entrepreneurial and business renewal. Thus, the physical location for, and characteristics of, a BTC must be determined on the basis of specific features of the area it is to serve. Already in Cork a number of private ventures have succeeded in transforming redundant premises, such as old mills, into thriving centres for small firms in a wide variety of businesses.

COORDINATION OF ENTREPRENEUR AND MANAGEMENT TRAINING RESOURCES

Cork, although the second largest urban area in the country, is at present very poorly equipped for developing the entrepreneurial and managerial potential and capacity in its economy. While there is a wide variety of courses offered by a number of agencies and institutions, and many of these courses turn in a creditable performance, the arrangement of courses available and their coverage, substance, and quality amounts *overall* to an inadequate and incomplete programme for creating entrepreneurial and managerial potential and releasing it, on a widespread basis, in the area. It is much worse for those attempting to found firms and for new and small firms than for the larger companies, who may be able to send personnel to Dublin to avail of the wider range of courses provided by a greater number of institutions, such as, for example, the Irish Management Institute, which are not available in Cork.

Many of the courses which might be put under the headings of entrepreneur and management training are geared primarily towards academic and professional certification of, for example, employees of existing, particularly larger, businesses, rather than the current real needs of new entrepreneurs and small, growing companies struggling to become larger and better. They are, in other words, largely in the nature of 'courses', to be taken for any number of personal or professional reasons, rather than a method of increasing the entrepreneurial potential in the local economy and improving the rate of realizing that potential in the Cork area. It is not, obviously, a criticism of the courses in themselves to say that they do not fulfill purposes for which they are not intended, designed, and operated. It simply means that overall they are not filling a need which it is urgent to satisfy for the improvement of the entrepreneurial process in Cork and, except for some courses which are contributing, it leaves open the question of whether they have or have not a role to play in that task.

For long term prosperity of Cork, new and small enterprises should have available locally to them, training resources, at the highest quality, focussed pragmatically on entrepreneurship and management; product development and marketing, technology innovation, access and implementation, personnel and organizational development, financial structuring and growth policies, and so on. To play the desired role, such courses, workshops, seminars etc., in these areas would have to be available in formats convenient to full-time entrepreneurs and business personnel (full-time/part-time day/evening, short/long etc.; group workshops, self-paced learning etc. computer-aided etc.) and made available by top quality instructors from local, national, and international organizations. As well as these it is vital that the experience and insights of local entrepreneurs including, perhaps especially, those retired need to be continuously tapped as part of the process of improving the entrepreneurial environment in Cork and sustaining it by creating a local 'tradition' of entrepreneurship based on insights acquired from actual experience of being in business in Cork. Possibly the main reason why the situation at present is inadequate overall, despite some excellent elements, is due to the fragmentation of entrepreneurship and management training resources which creates obstacles for entrepreneurship in Cork by allowing difficulties, as well as gaps, to occur. This fragmentation occurs because there is no umbrella or coordinating arrangement for the promotion, provision and improvement of such training geared to the entrepreneurial environment and process in Cork.

Thus, an arrangement such as, for example, a Regional Management Resource Centre, as suggested by AnCO/Industrial Training Authority (in its discussion document *Management Training and Development in Ireland*), could provide a suitable approach for bringing coherence and thrust to the available resources and stimulating the development of responses to meet needs not presently being met. Although called a 'centre' the Regional Management Resource Centre, as proposed by AnCO, is really a coordinating framework for effective use of existing resources. Except for a minimum administrative secretariat, and their necessary office space, it does not have its own staff or premises. All training is conducted by staff contracted from the existing institutions and organizations. It is the overall sense of purpose which Regional Management Resource Coordination would bring that is important. AnCO, in its discussion document states that it 'is AnCO's intention to assist actively third level institutions and other State bodies to become more involved in satisfying the management training needs of local business' through the formation of Regional Management Resource Centres. As well as this approach, which AnCO has made as a general proposal for any region, the Irish Management Institute is reviewing its programmes in the Southern Region and examining the training problems currently facing managers and would-be managers with a view to improving its effectiveness in the region. This is being done in conjunction with AnCO and the third-level educational institutions.

If a suitable coordinating approach were followed by the relevant organizations, which resulted in the arrangement of effective coordination among them, it could contribute enormously to the professionalism of entrepreneurship and the creation and development of new and small businesses. Such an arrangement is necessary to complement existing agencies as well as to meet the needs of the emerging entrepreneurial framework, specifically an Enterprise Creation Team, concerned with enterprise formation, and the Business Development Group concerned with further enterprise expansion. As part of their operations both of these would draw up business creation and development plans which, very likely, would include the need for entrepreneurial and managerial training of a high standard as well as manpower and business skills training. The planning for, and meeting of, these demands can hardly be done in a very effective and convenient way under existing arrangements.

The making of arrangements to coordinate entrepreneur and manager training is only beginning in Cork and, therefore, the operational form of whatever is finally determined cannot be presumed. However, it is obvious that, to be effective in closing the gap apparent today, it should bring together all the public sector organizations, concerned with training, education, and development, and the private sector organizations, concerned with professional and management training as well as representative of the various aspects of business, relevant to improving the entrepreneurial and business development process in Cork.

The need to be addressed here is not formal certification, diplomas etc., but improving operational capabilities in the areas of entrepreneurship and management of any individuals or groups of persons who want to be in business even if not, and perhaps especially if not in view of the current employment prospects, in a business already. Given the current economic situation, and likely employment prospects for the next decade at least, formal certification programmes are hardly the urgent issue from the point of view of the Cork economy. While these are obviously necessary and important in their own right they are concerned with different issues than those central to the matters being considered here.

Specifically it is urgent that, initially at least, special attention should be given to the needs of business formation, new enterprises, and small enterprises in all lines of business activity. In meeting these needs urgently there is no reason why all the resources to be utilized must be based in Cork. Indeed, the presumption should be in favour of drawing the best into Cork when needed rather than accepting lower quality simply because it may be available locally.

Since the working out of the organizational arrangements for this will obviously take time, some of the most urgent requirements could be met in the interim by special programmes which could be instituted under the auspices of one or more relevant organizations such as, for example,

AnCO/Industrial Training Authority, Industrial Development Authority, National Board for Science and Technology, the University College, the Irish Management Institute, the Chamber of Commerce, and the Cork Council of Trade Unions. Through special programmes they could begin immediately providing elements of what would, ultimately, be part of the Management and Entrepreneur Resource Coordination when established. For example, because of the desire and urgent need to promote new higher technology orienated enterprises in the area, arrangements could be made with the Training Services Department of the Shannon Free Airport Development Company to offer its 'Entrepreneurship and High Technology Programme' in Cork and it could, perhaps, be sponsored by existing local organizations and institutions, such as the Industrial Development Authority, the commercial banks and finance companies and the University. Given the way this programme is intended to facilitate the formation of 'entrepreneurial teams' it would, almost certainly, generate a number of possibilities for development under the Small Industries Programme of the Industrial Development Authority and could be assisted by the Enterprise Creation Team, if established, and facilitated in the developing Enterprise (Incubator) Centre. Then in a period of 2 to 3 years a few new, indigenous firms — properly organized, managed, and financed — could be creating employment in commercially competitive lines of activity and thereby contributing to restoring the prosperity of Cork. Slow as it may appear it is the route Cork has to take, and is already taking, and a coordination of management and entrepreneur training resources will be a significant step on the way if it is focussed on the educational training systems and resources which are relevant to business operation and orientated towards the current entrepreneurial needs of the Cork economy.

COMMUNITY AREA ENTERPRISE INITIATIVE

Once it is recognized and accepted that the primary source of entrepreneurship must be domestic then no area or community can sit back and demand enterprise to be brought into their particular area because that merely involves a transfer of enterprise out of another Irish community. That political game is not one at which Ireland can be a net winner and the effect of a 'beggar-thy-neighbour' approach is to bring about efficiency losses. Each area must become, so far as possible, a net contributor to the overall improvement of employment and incomes in Ireland. Therefore the question which has to be considered is whether each area or community can make a net contribution, in other words has it the entrepreneurial potential? and can it realize that potential by devising suitable community-based entrepreneurial initiatives?

The answer to the first question is a re-statement of the basic premise for an entrepreneurial approach, given in Section 3 above: in the absence of persuasive evidence to the contrary, it must be taken that the distribution of entrepreneurial potential, like any human talent, is equal across appropriately large populations. Therefore a feature distinguishing entrepreneurship between communities is the failure to realize that potential because obstacles exist, to varying degrees, in particular communities. So it is to the need to overcome these obstacles, by devising a community-based programme to create an environment conducive to entrepreneurship, that attention must be addressed and the possibility of doing so examined by, first and foremost, the people themselves, as well as their political representatives, and then the state and private organizations concerned with economic and social developments.

So far, the outline of the framework for promoting entrepreneurship which is emerging in Cork has been concerned with the requirements, resources and arrangements in a general, i.e. non-area-specific, way. For individual communities to benefit from this new direction for development it will be necessary for them to make their own community based arrangement which will effectively link with the general process for entrepreneurial promotion to make the best use of these resources for their own community. Each area will have some needs similar to other communities but also many that are special to itself. But there will be one fundamental aspect in common: the entrepreneurial approach developing, and which has to be developed, in Cork is not an approach which will be amenable to 'clientalist' politics for the simple reasons (i) that the arrangements are not evolving that way under the pressure of the constrained economic circumstances and (ii) such political manipulation would be easily seen as blatant stealing, literally, from neighbours.

It will be up to each area to *somehow* initiate and devise a programme founded on the philosophy of creating an environment for 'resident' entrepreneurship and business development and wean itself from the all-pervasive politics of re-distribution. In other words, it will be up to each community area to contribute towards a 'diffusion network' to spread the entrepreneurial thrust as wide as possible in Cork. To illustrate how the general framework for new small business creation is relevant to certain particular areas it is useful to discuss briefly some developments in the Mayfield area of Cork city. Mayfield is selected, not because it is regarded as in a worse situation or deserving of particular attention relative to other areas, but simply because it is convenient to focus on one particular area. But there are three aspects which also make it appropriate for discussing the early steps towards entrepreneurial development and the creation of a modern enterprise base in an economically less developed community. First, it is seriously underdeveloped so far as business activity is concerned. Second, there is the physical space and perhaps even suitable existing buildings in the middle of the area, which are suitable bases for indigenous enterprise development in Mayfield and, as well as these, there are branches of important financial institutions located in the area. But third, and the most important for the purposes of this account of Cork initiatives, is that the route being taken in Mayfield is 'low-key' and serious about creating an entrepreneurial environment and not one of political 'stroke-pulling' and one-upmanship by the people through their political representatives.

Some details about Mayfield are necessary at this point but they can be given briefly as the area has been the subject of a recent study which should be taken as basic reading by all concerned with the socio-economic development of, at least, the city and not just residents of Mayfield.[1]

The population of Mayfield, taken to be the Catholic parish area is about 15,000 and half of this is under twenty-five years of age. There has been a pattern of long-term unemployment and early school leaving, a lack of social facilities, and a fragmentation of the area because of the physical planning approach pursued. About a third of the families live in local authority housing. No significant manufacturing or service employment is located within the area and the major shopping centre is a mile outside the most populated part at Ballyvolane. The IDA industrial estate at Kilbarry is 2½ miles away across the traffic routes and the IDA industrial estate at Little Island is about 4 miles away.

There is a strong case for a better distribution of employment opportunities and incentives in favour of areas such as Mayfield. The will to work is strong and so is the expectation of parents and young people to support their families. What is lacking is a tradition of creating enterprises and a place to turn in the area for encouragement, guidance, and assistance. Consequently, ideas are not cultivated, expertise among unemployed people lies dormant, and many young people lack a tangible incentive to acquire skills.

A first step was the setting up of the Mayfield Youth Training Workshop under a local Board of Management with funding from the Youth Employment Agency and technical assistance from AnCO. This Workshop offers young people a place in the locality for obtaining very basic work skills, access to further training, work opportunities, or enterprise schemes. It was, however, a very small resource tackling a very large problem. It needed more and it needed an entrepreneurial 'spark'. In other words it was seen that there must be a local 'centre' that will release the creative energies of those who may have ideas, business expertise, and skills to create employment and to coordinate the assistance required to create an entrepreneurial and enterprise base for the area. The purpose of this 'centre' would have to be the creation of business and service enterprises which are *economically viable and, therefore, give long-term and continuing employment.*

---

[1] Donal Linehan, *Community Involvement: Mayfield,* Turoe Press, Dublin, 1984.

In response to the needs of the community and a recognition that there was unlikely to be any magic solutions of foreign enterprises arriving, each with a thousand jobs, a temporary working group, which also involves some non-resident persons from private and public sector organizations was formed in order to develop and establish a 'Mayfield Enterprise Initiative' to undertake the very complex task of attempting

- to set up locally based enterprises where worthwhile jobs are created and goods and services are provided for local use;
- to develop quality enterprises based on being trade competitive and technology orientated to avoid a dualism in the economic structure of Cork;
- to reach out to people in the area and to promote an attitude of business creation and, thereby, employment creation;
- to set up a forum for the consideration of new business and service initiatives;
- to provide advice and counselling on small business set-up along single proprietorship, joint stock company, or labour partnership lines;
- to support the training and product workshop for the testing of new ideas and the choices of training skills;
- to seek out local and national, state and European Community support for the local enterprise initiative for activities which are properly evaluated as commercially viable propositions.

In a phrase, the Mayfield Enterprise Initiative is seeking to create an environment in which *modern* entrepreneurial activity and business formation and expansion become integral parts of community life. To a large extent what is being attempted appears to be something new in Ireland. It is trying to go beyond the approach, which is certainly more usual, of trying to get some firms established or brought in on an individual basis and is, instead, attempting to get change on a community-wide scale which would result in a process whereby the Mayfield area itself becomes, directly, a net contributor to the business development of Ireland. This appears to be an unavoidable approach to the 'vicious circle' in which the many areas like Mayfield presently find themselves and which could easily become the dominant feature of the Irish economy, if ways are not found to overcome the internal and external factors which perpetuate the situation. It is not, of course, an easy matter to say where and how to break it, but it is also difficult to see how it can be broken, other than temporarily, if the local economic base is not developed. Without a local economic base there seems to be only two options: (i) as a residential-commuting area with employment in other areas or (ii) as a socio-economic dependent area because the jobs are not available elsewhere. Whatever about the merits or demerits of (i) the reality today is that the 'external' job-market is not, and is unlikely to be, adequate to meet the needs of communities like Mayfield, and (ii) is hardly acceptable on reasonable moral, political, or economic grounds, i.e. always facing the 'vicious circle' prospect if social re-distribution attitudes and mechanisms change as they do, for example, in times of economic stringency. Yet the reality is that thinking about the physical planning for communities appears today to be still dominated by the bifurcated view of residential and 'industrial' zones which effectively undermines the community basis for entrepreneurship. If enterprise is not a part of ordinary community life then economic and, consequently, social dependency is a constant threat; not every community can be a 'D4' simply because every community in Ireland doesn't have equal access to the controlling planning and re-distributing procedures in a political society.

Much is done under the guise of redistributing wealth. But it is not wealth that people get from redistribution policies. What they invariably get is current consumption — via state provided and administered services — or income to support current consumption. Wealth is therefore dissipated and not otherwise much more equally distributed. Too much time is wasted discussing the wrong issues about equality and inequality of incomes and in the — very expensive — chase to equalize net incomes. The real problem is the inequality of gross incomes and the answer to that lies in the process that generates gross incomes, i.e. entrepreneurship and enterprise. The challenge for policy-makers interested in income/wealth equality is to derive approaches that result in greater equality of gross incomes. Allowing and assisting people, with different income levels, access to the entrepreneurial process is surely an essential part of such a strategy.

There is, therefore, a need to address the unemployed directly by enterprise initiatives which are also necessary — as part of an overall approach to the employment problem — to bring the entrepreneurial potential of different income groups into the domain of effective entrepreneurial capability. This means that there must be a direct, active and integrated approach by the business promotion agencies and organizations to the growing number of unemployed, particularly, the largest number in Cork which is in the Greater Cork Urban Area. In effect this means not only addressing unemployment in general through the existing programmes but, specifically, the maldistribution of resources applied on the northside of the Cork Urban Area which is a pervasive feature of all the public sector services in Cork. Relatively lower labour skills and enterprise capability, for example, underlie an inadequate access to enterprise creation and development programmes and thereby result in the perpetuation and worsening of the employment and income situation in many northside areas. Of course, such difficulties are not confined only to northside and many other areas are similarly affected. But the underlying reality is that just about everything in the way of public sector agencies and organizations are situated on the southside of the city area, and, however serious the problems remain, it does nevertheless make a difference in terms of access to, and potential use of, these resources. And, ultimately, it matters for the overall prosperity of Cork to have this maldistribution discontinued.

But the lead in changing all this must come from the local communities themselves because, first, they must define their own needs, and second, recognize that the re-distribution game is not one on which they practically can or morally should depend in a passive way. On the basic entrepreneurial premise set out earlier, namely, that an appropriately large population is not 'naturally' deficient in entrepreneurial potential then each community must identify the obstacles which hinder or prevent the realization of that potential in their own area. The barrier to entrepreneurship is unlikely to be a single or simple factor; more likely it will be a complex of social, economic and political factors which will include, for example, schooling and clientalist politics.[2] Mayfield is an example of one community area that is attempting to develop a non-dependent strategy for its economic development. As it is very early days, in what will be a long process, and, most important, as it has to face up to new issues, following on the recognition that, if Irish entrepreneurship is the key to our future, it must be brought down to the operational level in communities like Mayfield, it would not be appropriate to try to document at this time the very early stages of what can only be a trial-and-error process of discovery. The working group is attempting to develop a coherent and comprehensive programme to remove barriers to entrepreneurship and to identify appropriate arrangements for the implementation of this programme. It has to face up to all the problems of entrepreneurship under the three basic headings examined earlier — people and organization; finance and premises; and technology and marketing — which are compounded by the lack of entrepreneurial tradition and resource in the area. The programme being developed is based on two complementary approaches to (i) address the short-term obstacles and work with the presently, or immediately prospective, unemployed persons to generate enterprise and (ii) address the long-term obstacles to entrepreneurship and resource needs for a strong local economy in which business formation and development is a matter of day-to-day life. As part of these approaches it will have to devise methods of linking into the overall framework for entrepreneurship as it is emerging in Cork, in particular the IDA Enterprise (Incubation) Centre, the Business and Technology Centre, and the Management and Entrepreneur Training Programmes as they are developing; i.e., to become *part of an extension network to spread entrepreneurship skills and new technologies* somewhat

---

[2] Linehan, work cited, pp. 21-2; 43.

similar to that which is common, and taken for granted as necessary, in agriculture.

The Mayfield Enterprise Initiative faces high costs associated with attempting something which, to a large extent is new and, as well as the direct costs associated with discovering an effective strategy, it can be expected to run up against the 'costs' of having to change attitudes of people internal and external to the community. But to seriously address unemployment directly in Cork implies a direct and long-term involvement in promoting business creation and expansion in the underdeveloped economy of the northside and other similar areas. And, if the Greater Cork Area is to be a low unemployment and generally high prosperity urban area in the next twenty years, such an approach appears to be unavoidable. There is no room for large 'underdeveloped economies' in the midst of what is, after all, a small economy. The overall prosperity of Cork is dependent in the end on the prosperity of all its parts. Thus, as in the case of developing countries or regions, the less developed areas of the Greater Cork Urban Area can be perceived as providing opportunities for economic development, based on *indigenous* enterprises, just as much as Ireland as a whole, or they can be ignored to the continuing detriment of Cork and Ireland.

7

The Framework — Further Issues

FRAMEWORK FOR ENTREPRENEURSHIP

There are, as emphasised, many developments taking place in Cork which will be important in shaping the future employment and income prospects for its residents. A few of these — and not, indeed, the most 'visible' — were highlighted here. They were selected on the basis of a structural analysis which suggested that in a time of economic adjustment, requiring flexible responses to changing circumstances, the entrepreneurial process is crucial for economic survival and prosperity and this, in essence, means people and organization at the local level are central to any strategy for the revitalization of Cork. In line with this view the aspects highlighted were those new developments concerned with improving the entrepreneurial capability and resources of the area as quickly as possible. For that reason primary attention was paid to the process of forming new enterprises at the smaller end of the size scale and to their subsequent development. This emphasis has come about in Ireland and not just in Cork, as a result of the issues which have got to be faced, specifically, the need for (i) an entrepreneurial approach, (ii) for any approach to be based on indigenous enterprise, (iii) to utilize relationships between small firms (and, more generally, small scale units) and entrepreneurship and innovation, (iv) to overcome isolation in the technology development and acquisition process, (v) for the unemployed to be brought actively into the entrepreneurial process, and (vi) to integrate the local branches of the major financial institutions into the overall process or devise alternative funding arrangements.

This gave a perspective which emphasised:

people and organization for business, finance of and premises for business; technology and marketing;

and, following from that, the new developments taking place or, in one case, of a type suggested to meet needs not yet addressed:

— Enterprise Creation Team
— IDA Enterprise (Incubation) Centre
— Business and Technology Centre
— Coordination of Regional Management Resources and Entrepreneur Training.

By calling it a framework for entrepreneurship I mean only that it is an exposition which attempts to make explicit what is being attempted already and to outline the connections between what might appear to be unrelated, or only indirectly related, elements by emphasising the two basic themes underlying these developments. The first is the promotion and improvement of business formation in terms of both the quality as well as the quantity of new enterprises; and the second is the promotion and improvement of the expansion of existing small scale businesses. Common to both of these is the attention to the people that ultimately constitute an enterprise, i.e. the entrepreneurs, and the process by which market opportunities are perceived and pursued, i.e. entrepreneurship.

The framework outline, reflecting the direction of change taking place in Cork for enhancing the coherence of existing resources for local enterprise creation and development, was not stated as a detailed or operating blueprint but only to provide an exposition of selected aspects which might contribute to thinking about devising effective ways to improve the entrepreneurial process in Cork. Indeed, it was deliberately kept general so as to leave apparent its relevance to areas other than Cork and, thereby, perhaps provide a framework for assisting thinking about the problems faced by these areas also.

As far as Cork is specifically concerned, the aspects emphasised here are *largely based on existing and planned resources and services* in the Greater Cork Area or on resources, for example, from the European Community, which are available to the Cork area. The severity of the economic crisis made apparent the need to coordinate these elements so as to establish a coherent approach to enterprise formation and creation in Cork. The purpose of the framework outlined here is to facilitate the local community, as well as the relevant agencies, organizations, and institutions in the public, private and voluntary sectors, to bring this about by addressing the issues which emerged during the economic collapse as needing attention:

— creation and development of good, soundly based small enterprises in all lines of business activities and especially with a potential for growth;
— focus particularly on the people and organizational aspects of business enterprises and entrepreneurship.

Because Cork is not the only 'blackspot', and not the only one facing similar problems and having the same needs for an entrepreneurially driven revitalization of its economic base, it is important to emphasise the point that the elements highlighted are based on the use of existing taxpayer-funded resources for enterprise creation and development in Cork. These are concerned, not with new programmes and major projects, but with implementation procedures for improving the coherence and extending the coverage of assistance and services to business activities not adequately facilitated at present in the area. The direction in which developments are moving reflect the present, financial and non-financial, constraints on government and, consequently, the shift back to the local level which, in turn, involves the supplementation of taxpayer-funded services with complementary resources from the private, commercial and voluntary sectors.

SOME MATTERS ARISING

Public discussions about what to do and how to do it, so as to generate employment, using taxpayer funds usually involve one of four positions:

— nothing needs to be done
— a new department agency, for programme is needed
— existing resources are inadequate and need boosting
— existing resources are adequate but implementation or delivery system could be made more effective.

The view underlying this account of the situation in Cork is reflected in the last two positions, most especially the last position. There is certainly a need for something to be done to increase the quantity of enterprise creation and development, and improve the quality of firms, at the small firm scale in Cork, i.e. to promote the entrepreneurial environment and the soundness of new and small businesses. There is also a need to provide and improve the range of services and assistance for manufacturing and service activities which do not meet current criteria for industrial policy support in the overall interests of a better entrepreneurial environment in Cork.

But the answer is not a new agency or department which in some ways is the easiest approach to sell, if it can be negotiated through the opposition that might arise from existing agencies for whatever reasons. The last approach — with possibly some increase in resources — is basically what is needed at present in the way of taxpayer-funded resources as far as the next most important step for improving entrepreneurial activity in Cork and many other areas are concerned. It is mainly a question of how to harmonize existing resources to provide a better focus on the particular narrow area of enterprise creation and development at the small scale within the total economic development programme.

Thus, for Cork, the main extra taxpayer-funded resources implied in the proposed framework can be summarily identified for the main elements:

— Enterprise Development Team:	existing resources (except perhaps for Borough Council personnel) concerned with enterprise creation;
— IDA Enterprise (Incubation) Centre:	existing resources as planned — some extra if enhanced or linked to BTC;
— Business and Technology Centre:	resources for preparatory work through the European Community — extra resources determined during that stage with possibility of EEC and Government co-financing etc.
— Regional Management Resource	existing resources except for small administrative requirements;
— Community Area Enterprise Initiatives:	personnel from local community on voluntary basis and state and private sector organizations as appropriate to their purposes, with other resources, reflecting the development requirements of particular areas, from appropriate national and local-authorities and agencies.

In putting forward a general conceptual framework, based on a view of the entrepreneurial needs of Cork and a selection of the developments taking place, a number of operational matters which inevitably arise have not been examined and should, at least, be noted at this stage.

One question which always arises when new ways are being explored and developed is whether there might not be too many 'structures' and 'cross-representations' emerging in addition to those already in place. The elements or arrangements emphasised here were chosen precisely because they are not matters of agency 'representation' as such. They reflect attempts to harmonize existing resources to focus on enterprise creation and development at the small scale in the Cork area and to bring the provision of services and assistance for this purpose more into 'line', rather than 'staff', relationships with entrepreneurs. Of course, merely setting up of Enterprise Creation Team and Business Development Group, with the *representation* of agencies on them, does not guarantee success. Success will depend on the calibre of the individuals selected, and, very importantly, whether a dynamic leadership for entrepreneurialism develops; so great care would, obviously, need to be taken in selecting people for their competence. It should not be done on the basis that people are selected as 'representatives' due to having positions or roles in agencies, organizations, or other bodies. The criteria is the skills needed by potential, new, and established entrepreneurs in potential, new and existing small enterprises, and meeting these needs is the all-important factor. However, the continuing economic pressures make it necessary and, hopefully, more likely that 'fiefdom politics' by organizations will not prevail in the years to come in Ireland as attempts are made to discover, by trial-and-error, the new instruments for promoting the locally-based entrepreneurial capabilty of areas like Cork.

Also, there are two aspects of the emerging framework, as outlined here, where the danger of real duplication and overlap must be examined. The first concerns whether there is a need for two separate teams/groups for enterprise promotion. Functionally, there are different needs to be met for enterprise formation and establishment than for the development of established enterprises. This is how the issue was outlined here. Whether organizationally there is a need for both, i.e. whether the Enterprise Creation team should be subsumed into the Business Development Group, is a question for which the answer can probably only be discovered by trial and error and by further examination by agencies and organizations relevant to the underlying problem. There are a number of points that need to be considered.

There is a functional demarcation between assisting enterprise creation and enterprise development and this was reflected in the way the exposition of the emerging framework was organized. This means, from the viewpoint of the Enterprise Creation Team, that it must 'let go' of new enterprises as early as possible and, from the perspective of new enterprises, that they are 'hived-off' to stand alone as fast as possible. The Enterprise Creation Team's job is setting up new firms as independent and commercially-viable business entities and not holding on to them. The incentive for it is to work closely with entrepreneurs but then to 'get rid' of them as fast as possible. New, small firms, on the other hand, could develop a vested interest, or at least a dependency, on being small if there was not a Business Development Group to which they can go. But if at a certain point, when they are 'hived-off' by the Enterprise Creation Team, they can see where they can go next they will be less dependent and, hopefully, more willing to embark on developing and exploiting their full potential. On the other hand, if the Business Development Group were not grounded on an essentially commercial base there might not be the same pressure on it to ensure the independence and commercial viability of clients. And the commercial basis of the relationship between clients and the Business Development Group will ensure responsibility and accountability for the services provided. Finally, the interaction between an Enterprise Creation Team and Business Development Group would provide both incentives and counterchecks for both in their efforts to provide the best services to entrepreneurs and small firms. Even after taking these points into account, the question — as to whether they could be part of the same organization, e.g. Business and Technology Centre, — would still remain quite open. But there is another dimension to this issue also.

If the Business Development Group is to be regarded as a commercial operation, why should the Enterprise Creation Team be seen differently? As pointed out previously, seed finance is a major obstacle for new firm formation and an important source — and probably the most significant in Ireland for quite some time — are state agencies and institutions. The manner in which it is supplied is generally in 'tangible' ways through premises, especially, for example, incubator facilities, training etc. Enterprise Creation Teams should be regarded as part of the seed capital for new business provided by the taxpayer through state agencies and complemented by the private sector which will gain from the new businesses created. Once a *firm* is up and going it is, by definition, a commercially viable entity and should be able to finance, or arrange finance, without, in principle, taxpayer subventions. Therefore, support at these later stages should once again be more commercial and more in the nature of an investment in, or loan advance to, enterprises.

Probably too much tax-financed resources go into supporting established enterprises, which could be done commercially, and the resources would be better utilized at the enterprise creation stage and to improve the overall environment for entrepreneurship by reducing taxation. Basically, there are two rationales for state help to private businesses: first, as a redistribution towards a business 'class' and related interest groups and, second, to promote the commercial base of the economy. The first is not an easy one to defend logically and the second involves the difficulty of ensuring, and *accounting* for, the best use of taxpayer funds because of the complexity and diversity of agencies and programmes. If the second is assumed to be the rationale in Ireland then, ultimately, it is meant to bring a commercial improvement. To ensure value for the taxpayer funding these services it should be brought more directly in line with commercial accountability on, at least, a reasonable 'portfolio' of activities, if not on individual projects or activities. The Business Development Group operating within the context of a Business and Technology Centre, provides one possible way for organizing the support process for small firms on a commercial or, at least, nearly commercial basis.

The second aspect of the proposal needing examination for possible duplication concerns the IDA Enterprise Centre (whether enhanced, as suggested here, or not) presently under construction, and the development of a Business and Technology Centre. Obviously, these could be brought together with the Enterprise Centre and its services incorporated into a more comprehensive Business and Technology Centre. There are many obvious advantages in having all under the one roof or, if not actually under one roof, then at least part of an integrated approach. Clearly, there should be no duplication — although it should be noted that the IDA Enterprise Centre can only facilitate operations meeting the criteria for IDA assistance and this has to be seen as a major constraint when viewed from the perspective of developing an entrepreneurial base to the local economy.

As well as raising a number of matters that will have to be considered in implementing an entrepreneurial approach, the framework outlined ignored a number of other areas, because of the emphasis on entrepreneurship and organization, that clearly also need attention to improve the contribution of the small firm to economic prosperity and employment generation. An example of the latter are the distribution and marketing problems faced by small firms, due to the scale demands of modern marketing, transportation systems, etc. It may be possible to arrange some form of group marketing and distribution arrangements on a local, regional or national basis, to provide small firms with the benefits of volume transportation etc. where necessary and to overcome the obstacles which individually they face in competing with larger suppliers and in getting products into markets. This places the infrastructure, especially the air, sea, and rail ports, and the services provided by the operating authorities in Cork, in a particularly important position and, as yet, one for which little thought or action has emerged.

A second example of the types of problems still to be addressed in Cork again goes back to the points about duplication and — no less important — gaps. This is the need for overall coordination to harmonize the services of agencies, effectively bridge the private-public sectors gap, and generally promote a positive entrepreneurial environment. There are, already, a number of representative organizations and groupings in Cork and it is possible that one of these could fulfill this need. But once again it is important to emphasise that it is not a matter of mere representation but the capacity and willingness to act to improve the enterprise creation and development process for small firms.

There is a very large number of organizations involved in the business life of Cork and each in its own way contributes to the overall environment of entrepreneurship and business activity. Some complement each other and some conflict with each other. Some know what some others are doing. And a few have no idea what anyone else is doing! There is no effective forum where the organizations and institutions most directly concerned with promoting, through small scale enterprises in all lines of activity, the business development of Cork can sort out the wider difficulties facing the area. Such a forum is needed, but would have to be done so as to be effective.

A third, and final example, of the issues still to be addressed in Cork is the virtual complete detachment of the second and, only slightly better, the third level educational systems from what could loosely be termed the entrepreneurial process. While it is not easy to say how it should be done, there is a widely held view that a lack of an entrepreneurial thrust in the area is, to some significant degree, the outcome of the overall educational process. In areas, especially of the Greater Cork Area where unemployment is heavily concentrated and secondary school attendance and achievement is low, the identification of programmes to ensure an adequate degree of competence in basic disciplines, combined with an approach that can be used for 'going into business', is necessary because they are the 'front-line'. Perhaps the 'one-stop-shop' for business promotion, established in Cork, could develop into a comprehensive business information bureau, possibly in conjunction with the BTC, and, as part of its services, provide a seminar/workshop programme for senior students at second level institutions which in the early stages could be based, among others, on the excellent series of booklets, *Your Own Business: A Guide to Setting-up and Running Your Own Business*, produced by the Industrial Development Authority. The third level institutions, in turn, could be major local sources for higher technology orientated entrepreneurship.

8

Conclusion

CONCLUDING REMARKS

After the experiences of the period 1982-1984 there is no doubt that Cork faces a major problem of unemployment and a declining economic base. Correspondingly it faces a major challenge to meet employment needs and re-vitalize the entrepreneurial process in all lines of business activity. But the unemployment problem in the Cork area cannot be tackled and resolved in isolation from the unemployment problem in the rest of Ireland. In the present economic climate, with the constraints on the state finances, any 'special deals' for Cork, to simply resolve the Cork area problem, can only be at the expense of some other area at best and would also involve further burdens in the Cork area. The employment crisis is so widespread that it is difficult to single out Cork as particularly worse off or more deserving of special treatment in the sense of fiscal re-distribution from other areas. Most, if not all, other areas could make equally valid claims for special treatment.

This, obviously, does not mean that the problems are not serious and urgent. They are, and urgent action is required. But Cork should not go for a palliative approach to the crisis. The 'long term' nature of the unemployment problem and employment challenge should be recognised and an appropriate response devised. The 'long term' nature of the unemployment does not necessarily imply that the problem must be there for a very *long time*. It will, if the response is inappropriate; it need not if the response is appropriate. Gains can be made surprisingly quickly by right approaches. If Cork approaches the crisis as an opportunity to change then the crisis and despair that were a characteristic feature of 1983/4 will also mark the turning points for a new era of prosperity. The crisis has brought a new understanding of the reality of economic life in a rapidly changing world economy. While the right approaches may not be easy to see in the turmoil of the complexity of changes and adjustments occurring, this realization should be built on to go forward rather than look backwards trying to continue as before until time runs out. The analysis and exposition offered here are intended to facilitate in turning crisis into opportunity.

This study has not attempted to examine all the economic ills of Cork. Such an attempt would be neither feasible nor appropriate. It has concentrated, however, on one very important area. In a time of economic adjustment, requiring flexible responses to the changing circumstances, the entrepreneurial process is crucial for survival and prosperity. That, in essence, means people and organization, and these have been the focus of attention here. Rather than bemoaning the lack of others' cash to give Cork a small and temporary fillip, as well as recognising the realities, a great deal can be done with what we have. While it is a time of crisis, it need not be one of pessimism or grasping. What is there can be the foundation for a strong, thriving economy once again.

Progress has to be made on a number of fronts and only a few of these came within the scope defined here. Most important is the general environment which must be conducive to entrepreneurship and organizational change. This sets powerful limits on what can be achieved. For example, much attention today focusses justifiably on the combination of direct tax burdens of administration, and accountancy costs, and uncertainty. The widening inconsistency between policies to promote entrepreneurship, particularly at the small firm level, and the imposition of an increasingly complex tax system is just one of the negative aspects of the current environment which requires urgent attention.

There are two economic policy problems concurrently occurring in Ireland. There is no necessary reason why they must occur simultaneously. Although they are occurring together today they are not the same problem.

The first problem is that of the state deficit and borrowing, particularly the unsustainable level of foreign borrowing which, combined with the use of these resources for current consumption and investment yielding low and even negative returns, has resulted in one of the most severe crises that policy-makers of successive governments have bequeathed the community. And this has resulted in extreme constraints on social action at a time when the demographic developments require the utmost flexibility and scope.

The second problem is the inadequacy of entrepreneurial and organizational capability, which is the most important resource limitation in Ireland, combined with a social and fiscal framework which greatly discourages domestic enterprise. The lack of a coherent entrepreneurial policy has been a continuous feature of economic policies in Ireland.

While they are separate problems they interact and compound the consequence of each alone. It is breaking this interaction which is the major challenge for policy makers in Ireland today and the crucial gap in national economic policy. Solving the first problem i.e. balancing the state budget, and even reducing the public debt, does not necessarily solve the second problem. And the long-standing nature of the employment problem counsels caution in presuming that it would. The urgency of the situation is such that we cannot afford to wait until, and if, the state budget is balanced or reduced before effectively addressing the entrepreneurial constraint.

It is necessary to develop an alternative approach with consistent policies which builds a long-term recovery from the 'bottom-up' — rather than the trickle down approach to economic recovery that characterizes the position of the present and recent policies. Doing this is not an easy task — not least because there are many crucial issues about which we know very little and because prosperity does not appear to be a condition which can be *administered* in a free society.

Compounding this difficult situation is the apparent incapacity to achieve significant reforms at the national level due, perhaps, to the stage at which we are with the bureaucratic, political, and interest-group processes combined with the simple fact that we just do not know any simple answers to the problems. Therefore, it appears necessary that we have to embark on a process of discovery, rather than operate on presumption or protection of the status-quo, and that the central feature of this trial-and-error approach will be attempts to devise local entrepreneurial strategies such as the one which has begun in Cork.

This introduces the question about what particular arrangements and organizations are most effective for delivering the services to promote and facilitate entrepreneurship locally. This will be an increasingly important matter in the future. Specifically, the localization of such delivery systems and the need to harmonize those provided by state and private organizations will require an open-minded and flexible approach so that, for the present, local initiatives based on promoting and facilitating entrepreneurship in all lines of activity, and for all types of firms, can discover new arrangements for existing resources which are suitable to meet the peculiarities of each area.

Thus, a re-examination of the distortionary nature of current industrial policies for agriculture, manufacturing, and some services, as well as the need for a comprehensive entrepreneurial policy against which other government activities and services can be evaluated, will also require a continuing examination of the state agencies involved in the process of business promotion. The Industrial Development Authority, to take one important example, currently fulfills two functions: first, it is a national agency set up to attract foreign enterprise and capital to the Irish regional area as a whole; second, as an internal development agency it is responsible for developing sub-regional areas.[1]

The question which will have to be considered is whether this is the best arrangement or whether it may not be more effective to separate the delivery organization corresponding to the two functions undertaken to meet different requirements, i.e.

(i) a national agency responsible for attracting foreign enterprise according to *national* industrial policy and *sub-regional* development strategies and opportunities;

(ii) autonomous sub-regional units, more directly linked to the local authorities and organizations concerned with development of particular areas.

Except for attracting foreign investment and removing obstacles to sub-regional equality, industrial or business promotion resources may be best left at the local level. Their use would be more accountable to the local communities which they serve and local communities could be made responsible for their own development performance. Of course, the arrangements used would have to be such as to avoid waste of taxpayers funds by unnecessary duplication within and across different areas. But, if the basic organizational form were a regional agency, then the means of funding would have to be different and would not involve direct power to tax residents in other areas for pure re-distribution purposes.

For attracting foreign enterprise, one national agency would appear to be appropriate so as to prevent multiple bidding from Ireland which would simply raise the price against ourselves. It can offer projects attracted by it to Ireland to areas or, when seeking projects abroad, work with, and to the requirements of, one or more areas to develop the best 'package' to attract the foreign enterprise. In that way local communities can decide what they want to do to attract foreign firms to their own areas. Correspondingly, the budget of the national agency could be related to the services it provides to the various areas so that its operation is tied closely to the development of the sub-regions. Any developments along these lines would, of course, have to be placed in the wider context of examining other state agencies, including the local authorities, as delivery systems, i.e. an *industry in itself,* and, therefore, in the context of an overall entrepreneurial policy.

But leaving aside at this point the particular details of arrangements which may be relevant and discovered in the futre, the important point to

---

[1] The following points are summarized from Connell M. Fanning, Public Private Initiatives and the Future for Cork: The Business and Technology Centre (In M.J. Bannon and S. Ward, editors, *Services and the New Economy: Implications for National and Regional Development:* 184-203, Regional Studies Association (Irish Branch), Dublin, 1985) where their context is more fully developed.

be emphasised in closing is that the last *White Paper on Industrial Policy* has really only opened up the examination of policy for promoting business in Ireland. However, given the long and difficult gestation period of that document, it is most likely that practice will precede official 'theory' by a long lead in response to the need to devise employment-orientated entrepreneurial strategies based on local initiatives.

So the key question which emerges to be answered over the next few years is whether the vast bureaucratic and interest-group complex, involving the interaction of private and public sector organizations, can be reformed or, where necessary, be eliminated altogether at a sufficiently rapid rate to meet the employment challenge. It is difficult to avoid a rather simplistic analogy with the dinosaur, when looking at the vast array of agencies and programmes geared to all sorts of particular needs — from manpower to capital acquisition as well as the enormous requirements which essentially are of a 'make-work' nature for many professions — and ask whether this 'dinosaur', as it has evolved in Ireland over twenty-five years, can adapt or *be* adapted to the wholly new environment in which the employment crisis must now be resolved. In other words, can the entrepreneurial-orientated local initiatives, spurred by the pressure of crisis, which are in their embryonic stage in places like Cork, push their way up through the layers of obstacles to become the dominant feature of the Irish economic landscape? In that respect the developments taking place in Cork, such as those outlined here, have a much wider significance for Ireland than just for the Cork area alone.

APPENDIX

Taxation — A Policy Direction

When government policies or historical accidents make the attainment of individual self-respect difficult, the nationalist spirit of the people become more ardent and extreme. (Hoffer)

The matters discussed in this study are not in themselves sufficient to resolve the employment crisis facing Cork and, by extension, Ireland. But they are necessary types of development. *An entrepreneurial perspective* was used to illumine the employment problem and identify issues that must be addressed. These, in turn, provided the focus on developments currently taking place as well as on their potential direction and their complementary nature. In this combination of *prescription and description* attention was concentrated on the 'local level'. But, of course, the overall national environment within which things can be done by local initiative is crucial and one question — that of the *devolution* of national development agencies to local bases — was raised in the concluding chapter. Matters of purely national concern must, however, be considered if these developments are to be effective.

On the one hand, the 'grant-aid' approach to enterprise promotion, which still predominates despite the recent *White Paper on Industrial Policy*[1], is increasingly subject to concern on the grounds of two simple related questions: *Does it work? Does it work well?* The answer is also becoming less confidently one of 'yes'. On the other hand, there has been

1 Frances Ruane, The White Paper on Industrial Policy, *The Irish Banking Review,* September 1984 : 45.

the need to devise policies to pick up the unemployment fall-out from the employment generation process which has been created in Ireland. Whatever the merits of these various schemes over unemployment and maintenance payments, which from the point of view of an individual can be significant, nevertheless they are largely internal re-allocations of tax-financed maintenance resources, which, from an overall perspective, are not a resolution of the employment problem, whatever the short-term effects on the unemployment statistics. The tension between these will have to be discussed more forcefully than hitherto and, as it is, the matters discussed here will be seen to be merely like the tip of the iceberg.

One of the bottlenecks in policy that will have to be broken in the next few years is, not surprisingly, in the area of taxation and its relationship to entrepreneurship and the employment generation process. Entrepreneurship depends, obviously, on individuals (but not, of course, necessarily working in isolation) and so the motivation of individuals is the foundation of the whole process. A crucial element in the complex of factors motivating individuals, so far as enterprise is concerned, is the financial reward for the effort and risk-taking. That is severely constrained in Ireland by the present levels, structure and complexity of taxes. Besides affecting incentives for undertaking legitimate entrepreneurial action they also limit the means for undertaking enterprise formation and development as well as employment generation. Ironically, in a society which is regarded as one that 'personalizes' every issue — individuals are blamed rather than the system questioned — it denies individualism, i.e. the *personal* basis of human action, where it is essential, e.g. for entrepreneurship. The tax regime is a major element in bringing that situation about. The result is that a statist or administrative approach is primarily all that remains or is permitted to remain and is, in the end, an institutional manifestation of a paternalistic disposition in Irish society. The dependence on 'higher authorities' and the like will not resolve the employment crisis. Instead of the state levies on gross incomes so state agencies can *create* jobs *for* people the resolution of the employment crisis will require a reduction of the income tax burden so people can *make* their *own* employment. Some possible elements of a direction which tax policy might take so as to facilitate an employment orientated entrepreneurial process are set out in this section which is entirely prescriptive

(1) A Tax Concession to Create Founder's Equity

There is a very wide range of financial assistance by many state agencies to private enterprise in Ireland. But no matter how extensive this range becomes there is always the need for personal, or at least private, equity-bearing funds to be committed to any business activity at its outset and, hence, for these to be saved in advance. The financial outcome of any business venture is by definition uncertain and there must be, therefore, funds committed on a non-contractual basis to underwrite the losses which could arise. This role is played by the ordinary shareholders in a joint stock company. Their willingness to bear losses provides some of the necessary assurances to other investors, lenders and creditors involved with the venture that the risks to which the contractual funds will be exposed will be kept as low as possible. It is for this reason that they exercise ultimate control in a firm.

This requirement is not fundamentally altered by the fact that taxpayers funds are made available through public sector agencies. Although the officials of these agencies are not placing their own savings at risk — and while they may have occasionally made or accepted unwise decisions — they are not immune to the same considerations as those of other investors and lenders. Nor should they become immune. Taxpayers should, at least, have the same protection as others if their funds are going to be exposed to loss and, especially, when their investments do not receive a direct return as in the case, for example, of equipment grants and training aids. In a private enterprise venture — one where the profits go to the private owners however little they may have invested — the assignment of unsecured personal or private funds is an important indicator of commitment to a project and an assurance to outside private and public sector investors, lenders and granters.

Personal funds are also usually an important source of finance for starting a new business on the smaller scale and, quite commonly, may be the only source of equity funds for some time. Public sector agencies, committing taxpayers savings to ventures whose outcomes are uncertain and the return from which, if positive, goes to the private owners, must be cautious and may not 'see' the opportunity or evaluate it with the same optimism as an entrepreneur. These agencies may also be constrained, or limit themselves, in the lines of activity which they can or will fund. Similarly, private sector lending and investing institutions and individuals may also have a different perception of the likely outcome of the venture. They both may be right and the entrepreneur may be wrong. But in any new business venture the belief of an entrepreneur, or entrepreneurs, in a project and a personal commitment to bring about its success is crucial. Because the outcome cannot be foreseen there is enormous scope for disagreement about the merits of a particular business proposition. Thus personal funds may be the only source of finance, at least in the early stages, for launching a new venture which, due to the dedication of the entrepreneur, may turn out to be a success.

It is not desirable, in private enterprise ventures, that the only source of *negative* residual or equity-bearing finance should be taxpayers savings (directly in the case of grant-aid agencies and indirectly in the case of

TABLE A.1

Percentage of Taxpayers with Marginal Tax Rates above 35% and 60% and higher in Ireland* and Selected OECD Countries.

Country	*Percentage of tax-payers with marginal rate above 35% (%)*	*Percentage of tax-payers with marginal rate of 60% or higher (%)*
Austria (1976)	10·2	0·0 [a]
Canada (1978)	1·4	Nil
Denmark (1978)	4·2	Nil
*Ireland (1978-79)	*14·9	*5·0
*Ireland (1983-84) [b]	*40·0	*9·0
Netherlands (1975)	16·8	1·7
Norway (1975)	7·4	Nil
Sweden (1981)	12·4	Nil
United Kingdom (1977-78)	5·2	1·3
United States (1977)	11·9	0·3

Source: Donal de Buitleir, The Report of the Commission on Taxation — One Year After, *Irish Banking Review,* September 1983: 28, Table 1 (No title).

Notes: (a) The share of taxpayers is less than 0·05 per cent, but there are taxpayers charged at rates of 60 per cent and higher.

(b) Estimate.

guaranteed lending institutions) or that business ventures cannot be financed unless meeting with the approval of state agencies or other large institutional investors. There can be little question that a typical waged or salaried income earner would find it exceedingly difficult, if not virtually impossible, given the combination of low income levels, the direct taxation burden and the cost-of-living (including indirect taxation) to accumulate capital for a significant business venture over a reasonable period of time and, at the same time, maintain a reasonable standard of living.

One indication of the position is given in Table A.1 which shows Ireland, for the period for which the data is most comparable, having 5% of taxpayers with a marginal tax rate of 60% or higher whereas the next nearest countries are the Netherlands with only 1.7% and the United Kingdom with 1.3%. Even more telling is the 40% of taxpayers with marginal tax rates at 35% or higher compared to the next nearest, Netherlands, with about

17%. While such data are only indicative they are nevertheless *strongly indicative* that, bearing in mind Irish income levels and cost-of-living, at best only persons with quite substantial incomes (and ignoring those evading taxes) could personally save the financial resources for a significant entrepreneurial undertaking.

While the tax concessions to promote business are apparently coming with increasing frequency they are invariably geared for people who already have high incomes and substantial funds for investment to make it worthwhile to tackle the inevitable complexity of such schemes. Few, if any, are really aimed at the 'average income earner' and hence the largest part of the population. This limits the supply of entrepreneurs.

To facilitate and attract ordinary wage and salaried income earners towards entrepreneurial activity it is desirable that an appropriate income tax concession scheme to *encourage and facilitate capital formation for the purpose of founding enterprises* be instituted until such time as the combination of Irish income levels, tax burdens and cost-of-living as well as the state of unemployment make it unnecessary. Such a scheme could be based on the features outlined in Table A.2.[2] It is important that such a scheme be kept as simple as possible and free of unnecessary accountancy and legal complexities.

(2) A Non-Discriminatory Employment-Orientated Business Tax

The need to resolve the employment problem has resulted in an active and extensive programme of assistance to *some* industries and enterprises. But, since Ireland has no option but to be a competitive trading economy, all sectors must contribute to improving the competitive position continually. Thus, since the task is to promote competitiveness in a market economy that purpose really identifies the activities and enterprises for assistance and promotion. These are the *competitive* sectors — the sectors of the Irish economy open to competition, i.e. open to entry by new firms of any type and entrepreneurs and not restricted by licensing (as distinct from certification), monopoly, cartels (whether privately or state enforced) or provided assistance through protection or subsidization.

If entrepreneurial policy is to be open and non-discriminatory among types of firms and lines of activity — provided they contribute to overall competitiveness — then an active approach to assisting enterprise will have to discover new fiscal instruments to meet this task. The old instruments of subsidizing capital are neither appropriate nor feasible for a comprehensive policy to promote entrepreneurship. If such a policy were 'successful'

[2] This is summarized from Connell M. Fanning, *Cork Towards 800: Crisis and Opportunity,* DOC XVI/350/84 — EN, European Commission, Brussels, June 1984, Appendix 3.

there would be too many enterprises to assist and the resource demands would be too great. Also, if we exclude foreign borrowing, some sectors have to be net contributors to finance these programmes. So there is compulsory redistribution involved: the so-called 'traditional' or 'declining industries' are excluded from support schemes; but they are taxed to support the 'new industries' and agencies facilitating them and these taxes in turn

TABLE A.2

Proposal for an Enterprise Investment Bond

1. Any person to be able to save any (variable) portion of wage or salary income, reported for tax purposes, in designated *Enterprise Investment Bonds*. The savings to be done in any manner convenient to the saver and deposit institutions. The amount saved during a particular financial year to be consolidated in suitable units of Enterprise Investment Bonds dated for that year.
2. The amount so invested each year to be *fully deductable* for tax purposes, i.e. prior to the levying of all gross income levies, income taxation and similar charges for a period of up to about eight years which would be necessary to allow significant accumulation.
3. The additional tax which would have been paid if that amount of income had not been saved in Enterprise Investment Bonds and, therefore, included (along with interest earned on the deposit) in annual taxable income to be computed and recorded annually. If a full-time business venture is not established during the designated period for each dated bond, or on the basis of the funds thus accumulated, this tax liability to be then paid over to the tax authorities by the deposit institution whenever the saver cashes in any Enterprise Investment Bond or on maturation of a Bond.
4. If a full-time business venture is established on the basis of the funds so accumulated and within the designated period for the dated bonds the tax liability to be cancelled. The funds accumulated for establishing a business therefore are the accumulated principal saved, the accumulated interest paid by the deposit institution, and the tax liability (on the income saved and interest earned on it) foregone by the tax authorities.
5. Because of the importance of establishing a track record with lending institutions the institutions designated for the Enterprise Investment Bond scheme should be confined to those financial institutions involved in financing business activities at the smaller end of the scale but that it be open to any of these so that, as much as possible, competition prevails in the rates offered to depositiors in Enterprise Investment Bonds.
6. Because of the increasing necessity for unemployed workers to create their own jobs by founding or taking over enterprises, workers should be able to invest redundancy payments in Enterprise Investment Bonds on equivalent terms as those saving out of current incomes.

contribute to their own 'traditionality', i.e. decline. Furthermore the differential risks and rates of return as between grant-aided and non-grant-aided ventures distorts the whole enterprise process in a way that is becoming increasingly questioned for a number of reasons.[3]

The foundation of an approach to non-discriminatory competitive assistance is to remove unnecessary administrative obstacles to all types of firms or lines of activity and eliminate all discrimination — in tax and legal codes, administrative requirements, subsidies and grants, etc. — among activities, enterprises and types of business organisations. No one type or size of organization is the most appropriate for every particular circumstance. A recognition of this, and appropriate responses from the public administration, would reduce rigidities and allow the foundation and growth of businesses to occur efficiently.

There is, however, a need, given the employment crisis, to incorporate *employment incentives* into the policy for entrepreneurship in a way that respects its basic thrust for competitiveness and non-discrimination. This could be done in a straight-forward way by treating all types of business equally and replacing taxation of enterprises, subsidies to capital, and taxes on employment by a tax on profits-per-worker in excess of an appropriate tax-free allowance.[4] A distinction could be made by allowing a higher tax-free allowance to the competitive sector than to the non-competitive sector. Furthermore, a graduated rate of taxation, up to a maximum of, say, 50%, could be applied to the taxable profits-per-worker (i.e. the portion of profits-per-worker above the tax-free allowance).

As well as simplifying the taxation of business incomes the employment incentive in this approach is that more employment can add to overall profits net of tax so that if a business wished to add to non-taxed profits it can do so by expanding the number of employees. It would encourage business to substitute labour for capital in contrast to the situation at present, which is out of line with the employment crisis. Thus the tax-free allowance could constitute the administrative or regulatory part of a transition strategy to full employment. When a situation approaching full employment is reached the tax-free allowance could be lifted or adjusted as need be so as

---

[3] For instance, Frances Ruane, The White Paper on Industrial Policy, *The Irish Banking Review,* September 1984 : 34-45.

[4] This section is based on Connell M. Fanning, Cork: Towards an Entrepreneurial Economy? Paper read at a conference, sponsored by the Commission of the European Communities, on *Innovation and Enterprises,* held in University College Cork on 2 September 1984. See also David O'Mahony, How Should the Plan be Interpreted?, *The Irish Banking Review,* December 1984 : 35.

not to operate as an incentive to labour hoarding and hinderance to economic transformation. In the meantime it could be indexed to the state of the labour market so it would change automatically. It would also have to allow for price inflation by being indexed to a set of representative prices, perhaps investment prices. Providing 'assistance' to enterprises in this manner would both reinforce the thrust of a policy for entrepreneurship and reorientate incentives towards the employment of labour as compared to the present position which distorts decisions against employment. Obviously, as a *quid pro quo* to make the scheme effective, it would be necessary to remove other barriers to employment, for example, the unfair dismissals restrictions which, among other examples, now hinder employment despite their ostensible purpose being to 'protect' employment: nothing protects employment like a high demand for labour.

(3) Abolition of Capital Gains Tax

The capital gains tax as presently formulated in Ireland constitutes a major obstacle to entrepreneurially driven enterprise for a number of reasons. First, the compliance costs are extremely high. It is also highly regressive as the costs of calculating that one is *not* liable for a small capital gain is the same as the costs of calculating what a very large capital gain might be. Second, it makes for additional uncertainty costs to a business because the liability for this tax is difficult to calculate in advance due to its complexity. Third, it gives rise to an important inflexibility in the entrepreneurial system as investors become locked into particular ventures. People who make gains are reluctant or afraid to realize them so that the supply of equity capital is made rigid. Due to the locked-in-problem funds are not available to finance new ventures by people prepared to undertake the associated risks. Fourth, it may be a de-stabilizing factor for the stock exchange which has seen share prices fluctuating widely on a relatively small amount of dealings. If people could go in and out on small margins then it would take comparatively big dealings to make small changes in share prices. But because people are not selling, except on death and inheritance, small sales may have disproportionately big effects on share prices.

The capital gains tax, for all this, brings in little revenue for the central Exchequer. The only important beneficiaries are the accounting profession and the Revenue Commissioners in terms of the business they do with each other and the employment thereby involved. Other than this 'make-work' aspect — which can hardly be advanced in its support — it is difficult to see how a persuasive case can be made for the retention of the capital gains tax and plenty of reasons for its abolition in the midst of the greatest employment crisis faced by the country. If, however, it is not politically possible at present to abolish the capital gains tax entirely, it should at least, and with a sense of urgency, be abolished on *founder's equity,* i.e. on any gains resulting from the sale of shares in a business by its founders so that people who have successfully founded an enterprise already can go on to try to do it again, and, thereby, generate 'real' employment.

(4) Government Expenditure Norm

Perhaps the single most important lesson that emerges from the stark realities of the present economic crisis is about how we got into such a mess. One outstanding feature, which has been increasingly recognized in Ireland, is that the political process was and, in the absence of reform, still is incapable of containing the excesses inherent in the financing of public expenditure by borrowing either domestically or, most dangerously, from abroad. In the political competition[5] elections can be won essentially by spending 'packages' (carefully constructed to create seat winning coalitions of voters) which have their ultimate financing implications (carefully disguised by complex taxation and spending arrangements) temporarily postponed by the use of borrowed finance. But in the end the tax bill has to be paid by (some of) the electorate and the fiscal re-distribution game takes another twist out of the economic system on its downward spiral.

The realization that the game has no boundary rules has led in recent years to suggestions that it be placed within the limits of a budget balancing requirement set by legislation or, more effectively, a constitutional amendment. But the balanced-budget amendment has three disadvantages. First, it may be unnecessarily restrictive. Although the excesses of recent years has led, quite understandably, to demands for balanced-budget rules to be imposed on the political process, to make governments behave more like households which 'must live within' their means, i.e. 'responsibly', nevertheless, governments can and should do things differently from households. Otherwise there would not be reason to have or support government as a social institution. But the irresponsibility that has been a feature of politics in some recent years has, however, to be curbed. Second, such a rule does not address the tax burden implications of government expenditure (or, indeed, the burden implications of government *spending* itself[6]). Government budgets could be balanced at very high or very low levels of taxation. Yet this is obviously the central problem that has to be addressed. Third, it is not always clear whether the scope of such a rule would be the entire government budget or just the part administratively segregated into the 'current' budget. But, clearly, to aim a rule at only a

---

[5] O'Mahony, work cited, outlines a 'public choice theory' view in his analysis of *Building on Reality 1985-87* which is the latest national plan.

[6] O'Mahony, work cited : 31.

part of the artificially divided government spending account merely invites the 'books' to be juggled by changing definitions. No doubt such changes would be accompanied by much public fanfare that the government had more scope for spending after all because it had just been 'discovered' that some item, previously included in the current account, was really a capital item after all!

An alternative approach is to fix a limit on the proportion to which government *spending* in any year can rise relative to taxable income (as recorded by the revenue Commssioners) of the *previous year*, which would be taken as approximating national income. This limit could be set by legislation, specified in the constitution, or, on the basis of a constitutional amendment, particular limits could be determined by referendum at fixed intervals. Although it would be administratively more complex than a balanced-budget rule it has a number of advantages.

First, it is based on a recognition of the fact that political parties compete for government office primarily by spending programmes which are crafted to create winning coalitions of voters and that enormous leeway is given to them by permitting such spending programmes to be (temporarily) financed by borrowed funds. It is necessary, therefore, to first pin down spending.

Second, specifiying an expenditure to income ratio implies a tax burden and so, after some time, also pins down the level of the overall tax burden. The balanced-budget rule does not address the tax burden problem because it ignores the incentive framework, i.e. the connection between winning elections and spending programmes, in a context which facilitates (via debt financing) disguising who will ultimately bear the cost of what items of spending, and that spending is the key to political choice.

Third, it is not, however, as rigid as a balanced-budget rule and allows a government scope to avail of the advantages of borrowing financed expenditure when circumstances are appropriate. Fourth, it places limits, however, on the scope for the use of borrowings because, if governments make extensive use of debt finance, the consequent expansion of interest payments will take over an increasing share of the total *spending capacity* allowed to the government and, thereby, reduce its freedom for 'vote-buying' with spending packages. Fifth, it alters the political market since, as vote winning depends primarily on spending and spending would depend on taxable income, winning elections would then depend on policies to increase taxable income given a particular limiting ratio for public expenditure. The scope for a government, i.e. its political action, would then depend on the effectiveness of its policies in increasing taxable income whereas at present the decline of incomes has only a very indirect effect on political behaviour.

Since to be able to spend more requires total taxable income to be greater there is obviously room for *once-off* increases in taxable income by (a) redefining taxable income to eliminate deductions and allowances and (b) reducing tax evasion. But there is a limit to these manoeuvres and also equity implications would constrain pursuing any one sector of the economy while ignoring others. Once these have been achieved all that remains is for governments to devise policies and manage their affairs so that the growth of taxable income is encouraged or, at least, not hampered. Thus, the incentive framework within which parties compete for office would be one that forces government spending to be actually *productive* in contrast to the situation today where probably a substantial proportion of spending is itself a burden which is additional to the tax burden.

Addendum: Taking Politics Seriously

Much publicity is gained by political representatives and candidates highlighting the 'scandal of tax evasion' although, when in office, little capability is usually demonstrated in tackling the problem. But the really fundamental 'tax evasion' is by governments who introduce spending programmes and at the same time evade, by the use of borrowing, the levying of the taxes which will ultimately have to be raised to finance that spending. However crudely, the application of a spending rule would bring a connection between expenditure and taxation in the context of a publicly higlighted share for public expenditure.

Since the purpose of the rule is to change the incentive framework in the political market the basic rule could be modified by the requirement that (i) all political parties state, as a condition for registration and continued registration, the spending ratio limit they will not exceed and (ii) parties holding Dail seats/votes in excess of a specified number/proportion publish, prior to an election, a five year budget framework (the overall life of a government) setting out the conditions by which they propose to achieve their goals within their specified spending limit. The latter provision is clearly in the nature of a 'public good' and it would be reasonable to provide all the parties which would be obliged to meet this requirement with an adequate grant to spend as they wish in the preparation of their Five Year Budget Framework. Once their spending limits were announced the emphasis would have to be on the *productive allocation within the global amount of resources available* in the political market sphere of the economy and not with the *continual* clawing of resources into it from the non-political sphere. In that way the political representative would have to face up to making choices about *alternative* uses of *limited resources* — just as has to be done in the non-political market sphere.

Public debate would reveal the inadequacies in such documents and this in itself could provide a very important source of information about the seriousness and capability of the parties. Providing an equal grant for all relevant parties would avoid handicapping new or small parties. The only barrier to new parties would be the need to think things through in a thorough manner so as declare their spending limit. As such it would have a stabilizing influence on the political process because it would only raise the 'price of admission' to the 'political market' by exposing the superficial 'public relations' nature of election manifestoes. Manifestoes are only advertising or product differentiating devices and their replacement by properly thought-out budget frameworks would signal that politicians take politics seriously and so, consequently, should the electorate. An expectation by the electorate that votes should be sought on the basis of a properly thought-out and coherently presented economic programme would signal to parties that the electorate takes politics seriously and so, consequently, should politicians.

(5) Concluding Remarks

The present state of the public finances obviously makes tax reform very difficult. But there are two other, and in Ireland today, probably more fundamental factors, namely, the dislike of real change and/or the lack of the capability to innovate and manage institutional change. The former can be made quite irrelevant by a major socio-economic crisis, so the latter is probably the most important and the most difficult. It appears to be a significant feature of Irish society 'in the large', i.e. at the level of overall social arrangements, and 'in the small', i.e. within organizations, that entrenched vested interests are able to stall the necessary innovations. That, in the final analysis, seems to be the real bottleneck and, consequently, the ultimate cause of the Irish economic crisis. As long as the past dominates the future the crisis will be with us.